Study Guide

to accompany

The New Managerial Economics

Study Guide

to accompany

The New Managerial Economics
William Boyes

Wm. Stewart Mounts, Jr.
Mercer University

SOUTH-WESTERN
CENGAGE Learning

Australia • Brazil • Japan • Korea • Mexico • Singapore • Spain • United Kingdom • United States

SOUTH-WESTERN
CENGAGE Learning

Study Guide to Accompany: The New Managerial Economics
William Boyes

Sponsoring Editor: Ann West

Editorial Associate: Tonya Lobato

Manufacturing Coordinator: Marie Barnes

Executive Marketing Manager: Andy Fisher

For product information and technology assistance, contact us at
Cengage Learning Customer & Sales Support, 1-800-354-9706

For permission to use material from this text or product,
submit all requests online at **www.cengage.com/permissions**
Further permissions questions can be emailed to
permissionrequest@cengage.com

ISBN-13: 978-0-618-32465-1

ISBN-10: 0-618-32465-8

South-Western
5191 Natorp Boulevard
Mason, OH 45040
USA

Cengage Learning is a leading provider of customized learning solutions with office locations around the globe, including Singapore, the United Kingdom, Australia, Mexico, Brazil, and Japan. Locate your local office at **www.cengage.com/global**

Cengage Learning products are represented in Canada by Nelson Education, Ltd.

To learn more about South-Western, visit **www.cengage.com/southwestern**

Purchase any of our products at your local college store or at our preferred online store **www.ichapters.com**

Printed in the United States of America
3 4 5 6 7   13 12 11 10 09

ED196

CONTENTS

PREFACE

The chapters of this study guide follow those of William Boyes' *The New Managerial Economics*. The best reason for using this guide is to help you learn course material and text content more efficiently. For each chapter of *The New Managerial Economics* this study guide highlights major concepts, provides you numerous opportunities to test your understanding of the material, and offers a case extension to help you apply pertinent concepts in a work-place setting.

Each chapter begins with a *Chapter Overview* and a *Key Concepts for Review* which introduces major topics covered in the text. The next section, called *Active Review*, consists of fill-in, true/false, multiple choice, and short answer questions. Each chapter concludes with *Extending the Case Study,* which offers you the opportunity to further apply important chapter concepts to the opening case of each chapter.

Every student studies differently and I do not presume to tell you how to study most effectively. However, the more you interact with the material in the text, the better will be your understanding. This can only enhance your success in a course. In addition, your ability to apply text material in actual managerial practice will be promoted with extensive interaction and testing. So, work hard and good luck.

Wm. Stewart Mounts, Jr.
Mercer University

Study Guide

to accompany

The New Managerial Economics

CHAPTER 1

Economics and Management

CHAPTER OVERVIEW

It is hard to identify the reasons why some businesses fail and why some succeed. Each possible factor (luck, market share, first to the market, etc.) has its own constituency of advocates. Yet, no one thing stands out across the population of firms. What does stand out, however, is that all business managers must make decisions and solve problems. Economics offers a framework for managers to better understand human behavior, and as such, analyze business issues. Thus, economics is a way to think. One of the basic foundations of economic thinking is that all decisions have costs. When one thing is selected, another thing is given up. The reason for this is that business resources are limited. This is to say, economic analysis encourages business managers to think in terms of alternatives when addressing business issues.

KEY CONCEPTS FOR REVIEW

core competency

market share

total quality management

ACTIVE REVIEW

Completion Questions

1. _____ often plays a part in a businesses success. However, to rely on it overlooks the fact that it is typically not the primary factor in a firm's performance.

2. The first firm to bring out a new product have been referred to as _____.

3. Scale and _____ are often thought of as reasons for business success. Often company size is the result of _____ and _____.

4. NAFTA, GATT, the WTO, and the EU have been agreements between the governments of countries to lower trade barriers. These have promoted _____ among many companies.

5. Many times, popular business concepts are often simply _____ concepts and theories.

6. Economics studies _____, _____, _____, and _____.

7. One of the most fundamental concepts in economics is that every choice has a _____.

8. To "know your customer" is equivalent to knowing _____.

9. A business can't be all things to all its constituencies. This is because all decisions a business might make involve _____.

10. When a business does one thing with it resources, it must _____ other things.

11. Economic decision making means that _____.

True-False Questions

1. T F   Lincoln Electric used a guaranteed salary structure to provide incentives to its employees.

2. T F   Lincoln Electric was not successful in transplanting its pay plan overseas.

3. T F   Being a "first mover" does not always guarantee that a business will succeed.

4. T F   Successful firms have large market shares. Their size assures their success.

5. T F   Core competency and value chain are concepts that can guide merger and acquisition activities.

6. T F   The personality of the CEO is one of many factors that might contribute to business success.

7. T F   Economics is simply the study of how economies try to maximize GDP.

8. T F   Business managers often can be seen using economic analysis to make decisions.

9. T F   Economic analysis encourages managers to think about alternatives.

10. T F   Another word for alternative is cost.

11. T F   By focusing on a core competency, a manager is giving up other things that a business could do.

12. T F   Business resources are often unlimited due to easy stock market access. This promotes the avoidance of costs.

13. T F   Economics is a way to analyze business issues and can be used in decision making.

14. T F   Economic decision making makes people consider the benefits and the costs when examining an alternative.

Multiple-Choice Questions

1. Economic analysis
   a. has little use in business decision making.
   b. makes managers consider alternatives.
   c. does not consider the costs of decisions.
   d. is based on the idea that business resources are unlimited.

2. The most important factor in business success is
   a. luck.
   b. market share.
   c. being the first mover.
   d. having a dynamic CEO.
   e. not really known if there is such a thing.

3. Lincoln Electric's pay plan was based on
   a. corporate profits.
   b. market share.
   c. a piece rate structure.
   d. the inverse of the price/earnings ratio.

4. When using economic analysis, all choices involve
   a. profit guarantees.
   b. only benefits.
   c. accounting principles.
   d. costs and benefits.

5. In economic analysis
   a. costs are viewed in terms of alternatives given up.
   b. business managers are assumed to have all the needed data.
   c. popular management jargon assumes an important role.
   d. business resources are seen to be unlimited.

6. Economics deals with
   a. human behavior.
   b. choosing between alternatives.
   c. market analysis.
   d. a way to think about problems.
   e. all of the above.

Short-Answer Questions

1. What is the single most important factor contributing to business success?

2. What is the nature of economic decision making?

3. Suppose a hospital uses corporate resources to develop a hospice center for cancer patients. Why might staff surgeons be upset with this decision?

4. Why do business decisions involve choosing between alternatives?

5. Why is economics the evaluation of tradeoffs?

Extending the Case Study: Lincoln Electric

Lincoln Electric's success was due to the way it paid its employees and it relatively small size. The company was able to have a ratio of 1 manager to each 100 employees, whereas most manufacturing companies worked at a ratio of 1 to 10. Following the herd that was stampeding toward "globalization," Lincoln Electric acquired manufacturing plants throughout the world. The problem was that Lincoln management had never done anything internationally. Moreover, the compensation structure that had led to Lincoln's success did not apply very easily to other countries and cultures.

a. Lincoln Electric's piece rate compensation plan created strong incentives for its employees to be productive and to spend most of their time producing products. Explain how this plan created costs for Lincoln Electric's employees, which they tried to minimize by working more.

b. Lincoln Electric's global ventures did not fare too well. A reason for this was that their unique compensation system did not transplant very well. Does this mean that economic principles are not applicable outside of the United States?

ANSWERS TO ACTIVE REVIEW QUESTIONS

Completion Questions

1. luck
2. first mover
3. market share
4. globalization
5. economic
6. firms, human behavior, decision making and markets
7. cost
8. demand
9. cost
10. give up
11. something cannot be acquired without giving something else up

True-False Questions

1. False	2. True	3. True
4. False	5. True	6. True
7. False	8. False	9. True
10. True	11. True	12. False
13. True	14. True	

Multiple-Choice Questions

1. b   2. e   3. c   4. d
5. a   6. e

Short-Answer Questions

1. There really is not just one thing. Many things contribute to business success.
2. Economic decision making recognizes that business resources are limited. When one thing is chosen, other things are given up. When a choice is made, benefits are gained and costs are incurred in terms of the alternative that cannot now be chosen.
3. The staff surgeons recognize that the resources of the hospital cannot now be used to improve the surgical facilities. While the hospice will create benefits, the hospital is losing the benefits that improve surgical facilities would have provided.
4. This is due to the fact that business resources are limited.
5. Economics recognizes that when something is acquired something else must be given up. This is to say, by deciding to acquire one thing and not another, the manager is trading off one against the other. They are comparing the benefits and costs of one against the benefits and costs of the other.

ANSWERS TO CASE STUDY QUESTIONS

Extending the Case Study: Lincoln Electric

a. Lincoln Electric employees had a decision to make. How should they use their time? Under the piece rate pay structure, the costs of using their time doing other things was the pay they gave up by not being productive. The employees wanted to minimize this cost by spending all their time making products. Every decision had a benefit and a cost.
b. Everyone everywhere is affect by incentives and economic principles. What Lincoln Electric failed to do was to recognize that institutions and culture play a large part in determining a person's response to an incentive. The incentive that works in one place might not work in another. This is different from saying that incentives do not work. Managers simply need to find the right one.

CHAPTER 2

Exchange, Efficiency, and Markets

CHAPTER OVERVIEW

The discipline of economics comes from the existence of scarcity. Scarcity means that when one thing is selected, something else is given up. The next best thing that could have been selected is the opportunity cost of the choice. All choices have opportunity costs. In an environment of scarcity, individuals often find it in their interests to trade with others. Trade involves a decision about what will be offered to others. This is determined by comparative advantage. By exploiting comparative advantage, individuals are able to consume beyond what they are able to produce. This is to say, they gain from trade. Trade and exchange can be organized in many different ways. For most instances, organized trade around a market creates outcomes that are efficient. Markets consist of demand and supply which interact to create an equilibrium price. Yet, at times, markets fail (from externalities for example) and other mechanisms for trade and exchange will arise. There are also costs associated with trade and exchange. The existence of businesses and their structure are based on the recognition that market exchange can be costly and that an organization largely based on an architecture of command relationships may offer transactions at lower costs. However, it should not be forgotten that firms ultimately relate to others – customers, suppliers, etc. – by meeting them in a market

As will be developed in the forthcoming chapters, economic analysis treats market participants as maximizers or optimizers. Buyers will be seen as making decision that maximize utility while producers make decisions attempting to maximize profits. The framework of optimization will be shown to be very usual for many different reasons. For now, one reason is that the methods of calculus can be used to gain insights into the behavior of buyers and sellers. The purpose of the appendix is to introduce you to the ideas of marginal, derivative, and unconstrained and constrained optimization from a calculus perspective.

KEY CONCEPTS FOR REVIEW

production possibilities frontier, PPC	comparative advantage
gains from trade	efficiency
Pareto efficient	externalities
public goods	market failure
transaction costs	hold-up
architecture	reengineering
downsizing	outsourcing

vertical integration	**horizontal integration**
arbitrage	**law of one price**
demand	**shortage**
supply	**equilibrium price**
surplus	**function**
scarcity	**marginal relationship**
derivative	**objective function**
partial derivative	**Lagrangian multipliers**
constraint	

ACTIVE REVIEW

Completion Questions

1. _____ means that to do one thing, something else must be given up.

2. The next best thing that could have been done is called the _____ of a choice.

3. Just because a country has an _____ in producing a product, does not mean that they have a _____ in producing it.

4. When a country that trades can consume beyond what it produces, it has experienced _____.

5. Specialization in production should be based on _____ and not on _____.

6. Differences in comparative advantages between countries can be traced back to differences in _____ and _____.

7. The _____ is a way to distribute goods and services.

8. Alternatives to the market as a means to distribute goods and services includes _____, _____, and _____.

9. Allocation mechanisms not only distribute goods and services, they also create and system of _____.

10. When a distribution is _____, one person cannot be made better off without making someone else worse off.

11. Economists judge alternative allocation schemes by comparing their respective _____.

12. The market allocation mechanism is often judged as _____ by many people.

13. Markets often fail when _____ are present.

14. When the efficiency of a market falls due to the presence of an _____, the market is said to _____.

15. A _____ is something that can be consumed by one person without preventing the consumption by another.

16. When a cost is imposed on someone when someone else either consumes or produces a product, a _____ is said to exist.

17. A firm will become _____ when it is more efficient for the firm to carry out transactions between suppliers and producers internally rather than externally.

18. The _____ of a firm is often determined by the costs of making transactions either internal or external to the firm.

19. _____ results in the _____.

20. Within a given market, _____ will often occur to assure that the same product will trade for the same price.

21. Markets consist of _____ and _____.

22. The law of demand states that there is a _____ relationship between price and quantity demanded.

23. Changes in the determinants of demand cause the demand curve to _____ within the graphing space. Changes in price, however, cause a movement _____ a given demand curve.

24. The law of supply states that there is a _____ relationship between price and quantity supplied.

25. _____ and _____ cause the price in the market to adjust and ultimately lead to _____.

26. A _____ is a rule that describes the relation between variables.

27. The terms _____ and _____ mean change.

28. The concept of marginal can also be symbolized as a _____.

29. If everything else is held constant, then the _____ is the change in the dependent variable with respect to a very small change in an independent variable.

30. The _____ is used when dealing with constrained optimization.

True-False Questions

1. T   F   Scarcity forces choice.

2. T   F   Opportunity cost refers to the alternative that is given up.

3. T   F   Specialization should be based on absolute advantage.

4. T   F   It is possible to have an absolute advantage in everything but a comparative advantage in only a few.

5. T F   Productivity differences between countries have little to do with comparative advantage.

6. T F   The production possibilities curve shows that a country can only consume what it produces.

7. T F   Differences in productivity are not a result of differences in technology between countries.

8. T F   The market system is a mechanism to distribute goods and services between alternative users.

9. T F   A random distribution of goods does not create an incentive system.

10. T F   A market allocation scheme does nothing to create production incentives.

11. T F   If one person can be made better off by a different distribution of goods and no one else is made worse off, then the allocation is Pareto efficient.

12. T F   A consumer of a public good cannot block others from consuming it.

13. T F   Negative and positive externalities can lead to market failure.

14. T F   Horizontally integrated firms find it cheaper to access internal parallel suppliers than external ones.

15. T F   The architecture of a business is, in part, market determined.

16. T F   Market boundaries are partially determined by the ability of consumers to substitute in consumption.

17. T F   The law of one price is based on the idea that arbitrage is ineffective.

18. T F   An equilibrium price equates demand and supply.

19. T F   Demand curves show what buyers are willing and able to buy at each price within some period of time.

20. T F   An increase in consumer income will lead to a higher equilibrium price, all other things constant.

21. T F   The law of supply states that there is a negative relationship between price and quantity supplied.

22. T F   A function describes the relationship between two variables.

23. T F   Derivative is the same as total.

24. T F   At a maximum or a minimum of a function, the derivative is equal to zero.

25. T F   The use of Lagrangian multipliers allows us to ignore the problem of scarcity.

Multiple-Choice Questions

1. All choices have an (a)
   a. absolute advantage.
   b. opportunity cost.
   c. comparative advantage.
   d. cost in terms of dollars.

2. If trade were based only on the ability of a country to produce goods,
   a. only opportunity costs would matter.
   b. only comparative advantage would matter.
   c. only absolute advantage would matter.
   d. countries would never trade.

3. Comparative advantage measures the ability to produce in terms of
   a. opportunity costs.
   b. the absolute ability to produce goods.
   c. the inverse of the production possibilities curve.
   d. the demand for a product.

4. The source of a country's comparative advantage is usually found in terms of its
   a. diversity of its labor pool.
   b. productivity and technology.
   c. imports.
   d. supply of natural resources.

5. Possible allocation schemes use
   a. the market.
   b. government decree.
   c. random selection.
   d. All of the above.
   e. None of the above.

6. Which allocation scheme creates an incentive to produce?
   a. The market mechanism.
   b. Government decree.
   c. Random selection.
   d. All of the above encourage participants to produce.

7. If economists wanted to judge the various allocation mechanisms, they would use
   a. the fairness of each mechanism.
   b. the popularity of each mechanism.
   c. the efficiency of each mechanism.
   d. the quality of each mechanism.

8. Pareto efficient allocation means
   a. that a different allocation would make everyone better off.
   b. that a different allocation would make the government better off.
   c. that a different allocation would make some better off but only by making some others worse off.
   d. that the distribution is unfair to everyone.

9. Examples of where the market might fail include
   a. negative externalities.
   b. positive externalities.
   c. public goods.
   d. All are sources of market failure.

10. The Lojack antitheft device produced
    a. positive externalities.
    b. negative externalities.
    c. a public good.
    d. raised revenue for the Boston government.

11. A lighthouse would be an example of a
    a. negative externality.
    b. public good.
    c. positive externality.
    d. profit opportunity for a private business.

12. To an economist, the architecture of a business is, in large part, determined by
    a. the availability of outsourcing.
    b. the costs and benefits of some activity internal to the business relative to the costs and benefits offered by external suppliers.
    c. the popularity of reengineering.
    d. the probability of a hold-up.

13. When a firm finds that it is more efficient for it to carry out transactions between suppliers and producers internally, it will probably be
    a. horizontally integrated.
    b. reengineered.
    c. vertically integrated.
    d. outsourced.

14. What has the internet done to market boundaries?
    a. Reduced them.
    b. Had no effect on boundaries.
    c. It made it more expensive for consumers to find substitutes.
    d. Expanded them.

15. When someone buys a product in an area for a low price and then sells it in another for a higher price, they are engaging in
    a. arbitrage.
    b. outsourcing.
    c. reengineering.
    d. an illegal activity.

16. Which of the following is a not a determinant of demand?
    a. Income.
    b. Price of the product.
    c. Tastes.
    d. Prices of other goods.
    e. All are determinants of demand.

17. An increase in prices causes
    a. a decrease in demand.
    b. an increase in demand.
    c. a decrease in the quantity demanded.
    d. an increase in the quantity demanded.
    e. both a and c.

18. Assume that technology increases and the demand curve does not shift.
    a. The equilibrium price will fall.
    b. The equilibrium price will rise.
    c. The equilibrium quantity will decrease.
    d. The equilibrium quantity will not change.
    e. None of the above.

19. Prices rise when there is a
    a. surplus.
    b. shortage.
    c. excess supply.
    d. Both b and c are correct.

20. Marginal can be symbolized by
    a. a total.
    b. a derivative.
    c. an integral.
    d. all of the above

21. To find a maximum or a minimum, one needs to find points where the _____ is
    _____.
    a. derivative, one
    b. derivative, zero
    c. derivative, infinity
    d. integral, zero

Short-Answer Questions

1. Why do choices have opportunity costs?

2. In terms of the production possibilities curve, what is the result of specialization based on comparative advantage?

3. Why are allocation mechanisms necessary?

4. How does market allocation create a system of incentives?

5. What does it mean that a distribution is Pareto efficient?

6. Why might private companies produce an inefficient level of flu vaccine?

7. Why do firms exist?

8. What is the purpose of arbitrage. What is the result of arbitrage?

9. Differentiate between a change in demand and a change in the quantity demanded.

10. Differentiate between a change in supply and a change in the quantity supplied.

11. Explain the process by which a market creates an equilibrium price.

12. Are prices that we pay in a store equal to equilibrium prices?

13. What is a function?

14. How can we derive marginal relationships from a function?

15. Why do we used *constrained* optimization in economics?

Applications and Problems

Assume that you have determined the following information about the market in which you sell your product.

$Qd = 250,000 - 500P + 100\ I$, and $Qs = 150,000 + 200P$, where

P = price and I = income.

1. What procedure would you follow to calculate the equilibrium market price?

2. Determine the equilibrium quantity at the price calculated in (1).

3. What role is I playing?

4. Assume that $I = 10,000$, what is the equilibrium quantity and price?

Extending the Case Study: Procter & Gamble and Launching New Products

This case shows the interrelationship between choices managers must make and the realities of the marketplace. Even though Procter & Gamble is a firm structured around a non-market architecture, it still must face the realities of the marketplace when it introduces a new product. As stated in the case narrative, Procter & Gamble needed to define the appropriate marketplace for its new product. From the last chapter, you will recall that managers need to "know their customer." This is the precise problem faced by P & G and the launching of its new product. Did it understand the willingness of European consumers to substitute? Did it appreciate different rules developed by different governments that might affect its ability to create a national brand? The management of Procter & Gamble needed to choose between alternative market strategies, each with its own unique set of costs and benefits for introducing its new product into the market.

a. Initially, Procter & Gamble chose to go with the "Eurobrand" concept and its associated strategy. What was the cost of this decision?

b. Based on Procter & Gamble's experience, should the European Union be considered one market? Why or why not.

Appendix Problems

1. Suppose a company produces and sells two products, x and z, and that its total cost is given by:

   $C = f(x, z) = 8x^2 + 16z^2 - 4xz$, where x is its output per hour of the first product, and z is its output per hour of the second product. The company has contracted with manufacturers to produce a total of 80 units each, with any mix of x and z acceptable. Find the optimum mix if the firm wants to minimize costs.

ANSWERS TO ACTIVE REVIEW QUESTIONS

Completion Questions

1. scarcity
2. opportunity cost
3. absolute advantage, comparative advantage
4. gains from trade
5. comparative advantage, absolute advantage
6. productivity, technology
7. market
8. first come first serve, government decree, random selection
9. incentives
10. Pareto efficient
11. efficiencies
12. unfair
13. externalities
14. externality, fail
15. public good
16. negative externality
17. vertically integrated
18. architecture
19. arbitrage, law of one price
20. arbitrage
21. supply, demand
22. negative
23. shift, along
24. positive
25. shortages, surpluses, equilibrium
26. function
27. marginal, incremental
28. derivative
29. partial derivative
30. Lagrangian multiplier

True-False Questions

1. True   2. True   3. False
4. True   5. False   6. False
7. False   8. True   9. True
10. False   11. False   12. False
13. True   14. True   15. True
16. True   17. False   18. False
19. True   20. True   21. False
22. True   23. False   24. True
25. False

Multiple-Choice Questions

1. b   2. c   3. a
4. b   5. d   6. a
7. c   8. c   9. d
10. a   11. b   12. b
13. c   14. d   15. a
16. b   17. c   18. a
19. b   20. b   21. b

Short-Answer Questions

1. The resources available to fill wants are limited, not infinite. Wants have no ends, however. Accordingly, when a choice is made something is given up. The next best thing that could have been done is the opportunity cost. So, opportunity costs exists because wants are infinite and resources are not.

2. The production possibilities curve shows all the combinations of two goods an economy can produce given its resource endowments. It also shows what a country can consume. However, with specialization, a country concentrates in the production in the good in which it has a comparative advantage. This permits a country, with trade, to move beyond its PPC. This is to say, a country that specializes can consume beyond what it produces. It gains from trade.

3. Allocation mechanisms are necessary because of the existence of scarcity. Types of mechanisms include price, first come first serve, government decree, and random selection.

4. Under market allocation, the ability to pay the market price determines who gets the goods. Therefore, the ability to consume is based on purchasing power. This encourages people to provide resources that are valued to producers and to provide goods that have high value to others. By providing highly valued resources to producers, an individual is able to acquire a greater ability to purchase goods and services.

5. A Pareto efficient allocation means that one person cannot be made better off unless someone else is made worse off. Anything less than this means that the allocation is not efficient.

6. If someone gets a flu shot, it is unlikely that they will catch the flu. An alternative way to say this is that they are less likely to transmit the flu to others. So, if someone gets a flu shot, then other people are less likely to get the flu. As a result, they would be less likely to get a flu shot for themselves. The flu vaccine creates a positive externality. People benefit from flu shots without getting the shot themselves. A firm might realize some of the people who benefit from the product are not paying for it. It receives less revenue when there is a positive externality than if one did not exist. This is the case of market failure resulting in a underproduction of the flu vaccine.

7. A firm is an alternative to a market allocation mechanism. Market transactions are not free. There are costs to making transactions and exchanges. Individuals will try to find ways to minimize these costs. For example, suppose that a manager needs 100 workers every day. Should the manager go out into the labor market and hire these 100 people each day? Or might it be cheaper if the managers contracts with his workers to show up every day and avoid daily hiring costs? Firms exist to minimize market transaction costs.

8. The purpose of arbitrage is to make a profit. People who buy a product at a low price and then sell it in another market are engaging in arbitrage and hope to profit from their activity.

   The result of this activity is that prices for the same product will converge. This movement is inherent in the law of one price.

9. A change in demand is seen as a shift of the entire demand curve. This movement is caused by changes in the determinants of demand like tastes, income, prices of other goods, etc. A change in the quantity demanded is caused by a change in the price of the product. This is seen as a movement along a nonshifting demand curve.

10. A change in supply is seen as a shift of the entire supply curve. This movement is caused by changes in the determinants of supply like technology and the prices of resources. A change in the quantity supplied is caused by a change in the price of the product. This is seen as a movement along a nonshifting supply curve.

11. The process by which all markets create the equilibrium price is through the concepts of shortages and surpluses. Suppose that, at a particular price, the quantity demanded exceeds the quantity supplied – there is a shortage. This means that buyers are willing and able to buy more than the quantity sellers are willing and able to sell. As a result, buyers bid prices up. The rising price creates an incentive for sellers to bring more to the market (an increase in the quantity supplied) and creates a incentive for some buyers to buy less (a decrease in the quantity demanded). When there is a surplus, the quantity demanded is smaller than the quantity supplied at the current market price. Buyers are willing and able to buy less at that price than sellers are willing and able to sell at the same price. As a result, sellers bid prices down. Buyers then buy more (increasing quantity demanded), and some seller bring less to the market (decreasing quantity supplied). In the end, surpluses and shortages are the key ingredients in price adjustment.

12. You cannot tell whether or not prices in a store are at equilibrium. However, if the actual store price is not an equilibrium price, it will move toward it over time.

13. A function is a rule that describes the relationships within a set of variables.

14. Marginal relationships are revealed by taking the derivative or the partial derivative of a function.

15. *Constrained* optimization is used because all choices are made with constraints due to limited resources. It reflects the ever-present nature of scarcity.

Applications and Problems

1. At an equilibrium price the quantity demanded equals the quantity supplied. So,
    $250,000 - 500P + 100I = 150,000 + 200P$. Now solve for P

    $P = 142.86 + .20I$

2. To determine the equilibrium quantity, simply substitute the findings of (1) into either
    quantity expression. So,
    $Qs = 150,000 + 200(142.86 + .20I)$

    $Qs = 178,572 + 40\ I$

3. The variable I represents income. This is a determinant of demand and it must be known
    before specific answers can be calculated. Changes in I will cause the demand curve to shift
    and, as result, impact price and quantity.

4. Simply substitute 10,000 into the answers found in (1) and (2).
    $Q = 578,572$

    $P = 2,142.86$

ANSWERS TO CASE STUDY QUESTIONS

Extending the Case Study: Procter & Gamble and Launching New Products

a. The cost of the "Eurobrand" strategy was the next best strategy that they did not select. In
    economics, the cost of any choice is the next best thing that could have been done. This is to
    say, every choice has an opportunity cost. Opportunity costs are not in terms of dollars and
    cents. They are the opportunity that is given up. What did Procter & Gamble give up? From
    the information provided, it seems like a multi-brand strategy serving several different
    market areas was the next best strategy.
b. From the failure of the "Eurobrand" concept, it is reasonable to argue that the European
    Union is not a single market but many different markets. Just because the European Union
    has a common currency and is moving toward having a common set of rules and regulations
    for businesses, this does not mean that a single market is being created. Procter & Gamble
    did not "know their customer."

ANSWERS TO APPENDIX PROBLEMS

1. Form the Lagrangian function $L = 8x^2 + 16z^2 - 4xz + \lambda(80-x-z)$.

   $\partial L/\partial x = 16x - 4z - \lambda = 0$
   $\partial L/\partial z = 32z - 4x - \lambda = 0$
   $\partial L/\partial \lambda = 80 - x - z = 0$

Solving the first equation for l and substituting it into the second equation gives

$$32z - 4x - 16x + 4z = 0$$

or $z = 10x/18$. Substituting this into the third equation and solving for x gives $x = 51.4$. Thus, the optimal value for z is 28.6, which satisfies the constraint of 80.

CHAPTER 3

Performance

CHAPTER OVERVIEW

The purpose of *The New Managerial Economics* is to show you that knowledge of economic theories and concept is useful in managerial decision making. One of the fundamental issues facing managers is judging the performance of a company. While there are many popular alternatives for measuring performance (return on assets, return on equity, and so on), economic profit is a fundamental component of the economist's bag of tools. This is how economists measure the value added of a company and the success of its management team.

Economic profit represents company profits after accounting for all costs. Costs include all explicit or accounting costs incurred in the production of a good or service plus the opportunity cost of capital, an implicit cost. This is referred to as normal profit. All resources must be paid their opportunity cost if they are to stay in their current use. This includes the capital that has been invested in the company. The cost of capital is not that easy to calculate, but concepts like the Capital Asset Pricing Model have been developed to do so. Economic profit is closely related to shareholder value. In fact, a stock's price is equal to the discounted value of future economic profits using the cost of capital as the discount rate. By focusing on economic profit, managers are better able to effectively manage company resources.

KEY CONCEPTS FOR REVIEW

economic profit

normal profit

negative economic profit

added value

shareholder value

market value

NOPAT

free cash flow

risk free asset

accounting profit

above normal profit

zero economic profit

cost of capital

economic value

Capital Asset Pricing Model (CAPM)

weighted average cost of capital

beta

market risk

ACTIVE REVIEW

Completion Questions

1. Markets direct resources to the uses that _____ them the most.

2. The concept of _____ is the difference between the value of the goods and services produced and the costs or the value of the resources used in their production.

3. Businesses that do not add value will not _____ over time.

4. In order to keep a resource in its current use, it must be paid its _____.

5. Even capital resources have _____.

6. The cost of equity capital is the _____ it could have gotten had it not been invested in the current endeavor.

7. Economists refer to valued added as _____.

8. Economic profit is not the same thing as _____, as it includes the costs of all resources including an alternative return for invested capital.

9. Economic profit = _____ - _____.

10. If a firm subtracts value, it is said to have earned a _____.

11. When a revenue is only sufficient to cover all costs of production including the opportunity cost of shareholders' capital, its _____ are zero.

12. When economic profits are zero, the firm is actually earning a _____.

13. Profit beyond normal profit is called _____.

14. To calculate economic profit the _____ of shareholders equity must be known.

15. The _____ can be used to calculate the cost of capital.

16. The _____ of a publicly traded firm can be determined by knowing the _____ of the company's stock and the _____ of the market.

17. Economic profit is obtained by subtracting the _____ from the _____.

18. Economic profit equals _____ less _____.

19. Economic profit and _____ are closely correlated over the long run.

20. Maximizing shareholder value is often interpreted as stressing _____ goals at the expense of _____ goals.

21. A stock price is equal to the_____ of expected future_____.

22. Economic profit is similar in nature to the _____ of an individual.

23. The covariance between a stock's return and the market return, divided by the variance of market returns is called _____.

24. A _____ greater than _____ indicates that a stock is more volatile than the market.

True-False Questions

1. T   F   Markets guide resources to the use that values them the most.

2. T   F   When the value of output is greater than the value of the resources used to produce that output, value has been added.

3. T   F   The purpose of business activity is to maintain value.

4. T   F   Not-for-profit businesses do not add value

5. T   F   Profit that is earned in excess of all costs is called accounting profit.

6. T   F   The opportunity cost of shareholder equity is the cost of capital.

7. T   F   Resources do not need to be paid their opportunity cost.

8. T   F   Accounting profit is the concept that economist use to measure value added.

9. T   F   Economic profit is the difference between the value of output and the opportunity cost of all inputs including the opportunity cost of the owner's or shareholders' capital.

10. T   F   Accounting profit = economic profit + capital costs.

11. T   F   Value still has been added when economic profits are negative.

12. T   F   Zero economic profit means that there is zero accounting profit.

13. T   F   Normal accounting profit means that there is zero economic value added.

14. T   F   To measure economic profit, you must know the cost of capital.

15. T   F   There is no cost to using your own money as business capital.

16. T   F   The cost of capital is the opportunity cost of the owner's or shareholders' capital.

17. T   F   The cost of capital cannot be estimated.

18. T   F   The Capital Asset Pricing Model takes into account the volatility of the returns in a stock.

19. T   F   Economic profit = NOFAT + cost of capital.

20. T   F   The is a perfect relationship between economic profit and shareholder value in the short run.

21. T   F   Free cash flow and economic profit are very similar.

22. T   F   Maximizing shareholder value is inconsistent with the goal of maximizing economic profit.

23. T   F   Maximizing economic profit is a short-run goal when it is done correctly.

24. T   F   The price of a share of stock represents the discounted value of past economic profits.

25. T   F   Changes in the expectations of economic profits will affect the price of a stock.

26. T   F   An option is a choice.

27. T   F   A weighted cost of capital is used to measure the costs of capital when the use of debt to raise money is zero.

28. T   F   Beta measures the risk of a stock relative to overall market risk.

29. T   F   The CAPM model can be used to estimate the cost of capital.

30. T   F   There is no such thing as a risk premium.

Multiple Choice Questions

1. From the viewpoint of an economist, the goal of business is to
    a. maximize consumer goodwill.
    b. add value by maximizing profits.
    c. maximize sales.
    d. maximize market share.

2. If value has been added, then
    a. economic profit was earned.
    b. accounting profit was earned.
    c. economic profits were zero.
    d. an accounting profit was earned and economic profit was negative.

3. The use of your own money as capital for your business
    a. has no opportunity cost.
    b. is free.
    c. is tax free.
    d. has an opportunity cost just like any other resource.

4. The cost of capital
    a. is only the interest rate paid on borrowed money
    b. is equal to the risk free rate.
    c. is equal to the alternative return an investor could have earned.
    d. equal to the opportunity cost of labor.

5. Which of the following is true?
    a. Economic profit = accounting profit + capital costs.
    b. Accounting profit = economic profit – capital costs.
    c. Capital costs = economic profit – accounting profit.
    d. None of the above are true.

6. If there is an excess of revenue over all resource costs, then
   a. there is an accounting loss but a positive economic profit.
   b. there are economic and accounting profits.
   c. there is an economic loss.
   d. the company is not adding value.

7. To keep laborers working in your business
   a. you must pay them at least their opportunity costs.
   b. you must pay them the minimum wage.
   c. you simply tell them what you will pay.
   d. you can ignore the market wage.

8. If a company has added value,
   a. economic profits will be zero.
   b. economic profits will be positive.
   c. economic profits will be negative.
   d. accounting profits will be positive.

9. If a company has taken away value,
   a. economic profits will be zero
   b. economic profits will be positive.
   c. economic profits will be negative.
   d. accounting profits will equal the cost of capital.

10. If economic profits are zero,
    a. normal accounting profits are earned.
    b. value has been added.
    c. value has been lost.
    d. the cost of capital was not covered by revenue.

11. The cost of capital
    a. cannot be measured.
    b. only matters if debt is used to raise money.
    c. is independent of the opportunity cost of shareholders.
    d. can be measured by CAPM.

12. The Capital Asset Pricing Model
    a. calculates the risk free rate.
    b. calculates the interest rate on government securities.
    c. assumes that risk is neutral in business decisions.
    d. devises a risk premium that must be added to the risk free rate.

13. The riskiness of a publicly traded firm can be measured
    a. by comparing the volatility of its stock to that of the market.
    b. by the inverse of market risk.
    c. by the average volatility of all risky firms.
    d. a and b are true.

14. Economic profits may be obtained by
    a. adding costs of capital to NOPAT.
    b. subtracting costs of capital from NOPAT.
    c. dividing the cost of capital into NOPAT.
    d. multiplying the cost of capital and NOPAT.

15. A weighted cost of capital must be used when
    a. only retained earnings are used.
    b. only borrowed money is used.
    c. both debt and equity are used.
    d. only equity is used.

16. Economic profit is the same as
    a. free cash flow.
    b. NOPAT less cost of capital.
    c. accounting profit less the cost of capital.
    d. All of the above are similar to economic profits.

17. Shareholder value and economic profits
    a. are not related at all.
    b. are directly related over a long period of time.
    c. are indirectly related over a long period of time.
    d. are reciprocals of each other.

18. The price of a share of stock
    a. is the present value of expected future economic profits.
    b. is a multiple of sales.
    c. contains no real information about the performance of a company.
    d. is, on average, as volatile as any given market index.

19. Beta is
    a. is a measure of the risk of a security.
    b. is largely independent of a company's performance.
    c. is determined by the performance of other firms in the specific industry.
    d. is usually less than one for dot.com companies.

20. If the risk of a security is no worse than the general risk inherent in the market, then
    a. beta will be greater than 1.
    b. beta will be less than 1 but greater than zero.
    c. beta will be equal to 1.
    d. beta will be zero.

21. If the risk of a security is greater than the general risk inherent in the market, then
    a. beta will be greater than 1.
    b. beta will be less than 1 but greater than zero.
    c. beta will be equal to 1.
    d. beta will be zero.

22. If the risk of a security is less than the general risk inherent in the market, then
    a. beta will be greater than 1.
    b. beta will be less than 1.
    c. beta will be equal to 1.
    d. beta will be infinity.

23. The Capital Asset Pricing Model states that
    a. expected return on a security is greater than the risk free rate plus beta times the market risk.
    b. expected return on a security is less than the risk free rate plus beta times the market risk.

  c. expected return on a security is equal to the risk free rate plus beta times the market risk.

  d. None of the above.

Short-Answer Questions

1. Why does economic profit show value added?

2. How is capital obtained?

3. My uncle gave me money to use in my new business and told me that it was a gift and not a loan. No interest payments are required. Because of his generosity, I am able to lower my costs of production and record larger profits. Please comment.

4. What is the difference between accounting profit and economic profit?

5. Can accounting profit be positive while economic profit is negative?

6. In reviewing my portfolio, I discover that some of the firms in which I have invested had zero economic profit. They added no value and I am very disappointed. Should I sell the stock and invest in my next best alternative? Would I be better off by changing my portfolio?

7. What is the cost of capital and how can it be measured?

8. Over the long run, should a company maximize shareholder value or economic profit?

9. My brother the stockbroker, has advised me to buy certain stocks. He says that they have had a good track record. Plus, they all have current economic profits. Is this sound advice?

10. Why might a company's stock price be rising even in the face of continuous negative economic profits?

11. What is CAPM and what does it do?

12. What is a risk free rate?

13. What is beta and what does it mean when it is greater than 1?

14. How can CAPM be used to measure the cost of capital for a particular company?

15. What is relative market risk?

Applications and Problems

1. Calculate the value added of the following two firms. Which one has added value? What advice would you give the investors in each company?

Company A		**Company B**	
Revenue	$2500	Revenue	$2000
Wages	$1000	Wages	$2000
Materials	$1300	Materials	$2925
Capital Costs	$50	Capital Costs	$75

2. Take the following costs of capital:

Motorola	11.6
Hershey Food	12.8
Home Depot	12.2
Dillard's Stores	10.5
Coca Cola	12

   a. Why are they what they are?

   b. Why would they differ?

3. Why would a company's stock rise if they announced a loss from the most recent quarter?

4. Assume that you are faced with three options and the economic profits from each are as follows:

Option	Profit in Year 1	Profit in Year 2	Profit in Year 3
A	$7000	$7000	$7000
B	$5000	$8000	$9000
C	$5000	$10,000	$5000

   a. Rank the options assuming that the risk free rate is 5% and the risk premium is 7%.

   b. What would happen to the rankings if the risk free rate rose to 6%?

   c. What would happen to the rankings if the risk premium would rise to 10%?

   d. What ultimately determines the rankings?

5. Assume that the risk free rate is 5%, the expected general market risk is 10%, and that beta is 1.25. What is the expected cost of capital? What happens to the expected cost of capital if the risk free rate rises to 10? In this case, what is the role of beta?

Extending the Case Study: The Enron Caper

One of the business headlines that came out of 2002 dealt with financial disclosure. Enron and its use of off-balance sheet partnerships is one of the best known examples of managers and their use (or misuse) of accounting techniques to alter financial information that is revealed to shareholders and to the public. Enron is not the only example of this manipulation. WorldCom, the second largest provider of long distance services and the largest holder of internet infrastructure, revealed that it had classified operating expenses as capital expenditures. This allowed WorldCom to report small expenses and, thereby, raise profits. Elsewhere, Merrill Lynch settled a case in New York which alleged that brokers, purposely using misinformation and incorrect classification, promoted stocks which Merrill's underwriting unit was trying to sell.

a. What role does information play in the valuing of economic profits?

b. What impact might inaccurate financial information have on the stock market?

c. Do short-term vs. long-term goals enter into this case?

ANSWERS TO ACTIVE REVIEW QUESTIONS

Completion Questions

1. value
2. adding value
3. survive
4. opportunity cost
5. opportunity costs
6. alternative return
7. economic profit
8. accounting profit
9. accounting profit, capital costs
10. negative economic profit
11. economic profits
12. normal accounting profits
13. economic profit
14. cost of capital
15. Capital Asset Pricing Model
16. risk, volatility, volatility
17. cost of capital, NOPAT
18. NOPAT, capital charges
19. shareholder value
20. short term, long term
21. present value, economic profit
22. net worth
23. beta
24. beta, one

True-False Questions

1.	True	2.	True	3.	False
4.	False	5.	False	6.	True
7.	False	8.	False	9.	True
10.	True	11.	False	12.	False
13.	True	14.	True	15.	False
16.	True	17.	False	18.	True
19.	False	20.	False	21.	True
22.	False	23.	False	24.	False
25.	True	26.	True	27.	False
28.	True	29.	True	30.	False

Multiple-Choice Questions

1.	b	2.	a	3.	d
4.	c	5.	c	6.	b
7.	a	8.	b	9.	c
10.	a	11.	d	12.	d
13.	a	14.	b	15.	c
16.	d	17.	b	18.	a
19.	a	20.	c	21.	a
22.	b	23.	c		

Short-Answer Questions

1. Economic profit is profit earned after accounting for all costs including the cost of capital. The costs of production represent opportunity costs. This is to say, a firm must pay a resource an amount of money at least equal to what it could have earned in its next best alternative. Economic profit is value beyond all opportunity costs. As such, it represents value added.
2. Capital is obtained by either debt, selling equity rights, or by retaining earnings. Of course, any combination of the three is also a way.
3. While my uncle may be generous, he did not allow me to avoid a cost of production. It is true that I do not have to make an explicit interest payment, but I could have invested his gift somewhere else. As such, when I use his gift in my business, I incur an opportunity cost which should be included in my cost of capital. Only then will economic profit be calculated correctly.
4. Accounting profit is revenue less the costs of inputs excluding the opportunity cost of the owner's capital. Economic profit is accounting profit less the opportunity cost of the owner's capital.
5. Yes, this is possible. Accounting profit is profit after accounting for all costs except for the cost of capital. It is possible that the costs of capital exceed the accounting profit. In this case, there will be negative economic profit and value has been lost.
6. When economic profit is zero, all costs of production have been paid including the opportunity cost of capital. Shareholders have earned at least what they could have earned in their next best alternative. So, changing your portfolio would not make you better off. In fact, if there are brokerage fees associated with changing your portfolio, you would be worse off.
7. The cost of capital represents the opportunity cost of an owner's (or shareholders') capital. It can be measured many ways including the Capital Asset Pricing Model. The cost of capital would include a risk free component as well as a component accounting for the riskiness of the particular business.
8. Over a long period of time the maximization of shareholder value and the maximization of economic profit are the same thing. If shareholder value is seen in a stock price, then shareholder value can be seen as the present value of future economic profits discounted at the appropriate cost of capital.
9. While past performance of a company matters is some ways, what matters the most is the

expected performance. Stock markets look ahead in the pricing of shares and, therefore, represent investor expectations. In addition, it is the expectation of future economic profits. Current economic profits might be something I use in forming my expectations, but they are not the only thing. In this light, my brother the broker might be shortsighted.

10. A stock price represents the present value of expected economic profits. Past performance, while influencing expectations, are not the only thing that the stock market uses in forming expectations. In this case, the market currently expects future economic profits.

11. CAPM is the Capital Asset Pricing Model. It states that the expected return on an asset is equal to the risk free rate plus beta multiplied by the market risk.

12. A risk free rate is the rate of return that is expected on an investment that is viewed as having no risk. For example, government securities are viewed as having no risk. Therefore, their return may be considered a risk free rate.

13. Beta is the risk of security relative to general market risk. It is the covariance between a security's return and the market's return divided by the variance of the market return. If beta is greater than 1, then the volatility of a particular stock is greater than the general volatility of the market.

14. To calculate the cost of capital you would need to know the risk free rate, the beta for the specific company, and the general market risk.

15. Relative market risk is equal to a measure of overall market risk less the risk free rate.

Applications and Problems

1. Value added is determined by subtracting the costs from the revenue. The economic value added of Company A is $100 and $0 for Company B. Company A has added value. The investors in each company should stay where they are. At the very least, the investors of Company B are covering their opportunity costs.

2. a. They represent the opportunity cost of the stockholders of each of the companies.
   b. Assuming that they contain the same risk free rate, they differ due to different risk premiums that investors attach to each company.

3. If the loss was smaller than the loss investors had expected, then the stock price would rise.

4. a. Option A = $7000+7000(1.12)+7000(1.12)^2 = 18,830$
      Option B = $5000+8000(1.12)+9000(1.12)^2 = 19,316$
      Option C = $5000+10,000(1.12)+5000(1.12)^2 = 17,914$
   b. The rankings would not change. The discount rate is a constant so it would not affect the outcomes.
   c. The ranking would not change.
   d. The rankings are determined by the expected profit. The present value is affected by the discount rate, but the ultimate outcomes are not affected.

5. Expected cost of capital = $5 + 1.25(10 - 5) = 11.25$
   Expected cost of capital = $10 + 1.25(10-10) = 10$; The expected cost of capital is 10. When the risk free rate equals the general market risk premium, then the cost of capital is unaffected by beta.

ANSWERS TO CASE STUDY QUESTIONS

Extending the Case Study: The Enron Caper

a.   The examples in the book which calculate economic profit assume that a company's financial statements present information accurately over time. Remember, the calculation of economic profit is a point-in-time estimate. However, a stock price is the present value of the future stream of economic profits discounted at the appropriate cost of capital. This requires future information that is not yet known. As such, it must be estimated by all market participants. Company information is but just one source of information about its future financial performance. Just because a company says something, does not mean it is totally believed by others. As you will see throughout the book, markets process information. As a matter of fact, the stock prices of both Enron and WorldCom had been falling long before their imaginative financial games were revealed.

b.   There are probably two considerations. First, shareholders may attach a higher risk premium to a particular company they suspect of financial manipulation. This would raise the cost of capital and lower the present value of future economic profits, lowering the company's stock price. Second, over the long run, companies more aggressive in indicating the accuracy of their financial information to shareholders may experience a lowering of the risk premium attached to them, thereby raising the price of a share.

c.   Due to the presence of options, futures, and other choices, investors may find profit opportunities in their use. As such, there would be no advantage in having short term and long term goals that differ.

CHAPTER 4

Demand

CHAPTER OVERVIEW

In the last chapter we saw that economic profit is a very good measure of a company's performance. It was calculated by subtracting from revenue all the costs of production including the cost of capital. In Chapter 4 we focus on demand, the foundations of revenue or sales. Total revenue is the first item in the income statement. Given its definition of price per unit multiplied by quantity sold, total revenue is the primary way consumers communicate to a business. As we have seen, the relationship between price and quantity demanded is demand.

To understand the behavior of revenue, every business must understand the demand it faces. A primary tool for this is seen in the price elasticity of demand which measures the responsiveness of quantity demanded to changes in price. Its formal definition is the percentage change in the quantity demanded resulting from a one per cent change in price. It can range from less than one (inelastic), to greater than one (elastic), or be equal to one (unit elastic). More importantly, by knowing price elasticity, a manager can connect price changes to changes in revenue. Income elasticity and cross elasticity are two other concepts that managers can use to understand their customers. Yet, understanding the customer is still not easy. For this reason businesses conduct market research through things like focus groups, surveys, buyer intention questionnaires, and experiments.

The key concept of this chapter is that of price elasticity of demand. This measures the responsiveness of quantity demanded to changes in price. An underlying component of this is the behavior of individual consumers. The purpose of the appendix is to outline briefly the theory of consumer behavior. An important part of consumer behavior is that consumers substitute, to one degree or another, when faced with a price change. This is the individual behavior reflected in the price elasticity of demand. The appendix also presents the calculus of consumer choice.

KEY CONCEPTS FOR REVIEW

price elasticity of demand	elastic
inelastic	unit-elastic
income elasticity of demand	cross elasticity of demand
substitutes	complements
cyclical goods	noncyclical goods
countercyclical goods	luxury goods
normal goods	inferior goods

complementors   revenue management systems

market research   primary and secondary data

focus groups   buyer intentions

indifference analysis   indifference curves

budget line   marginal rate of substitution

framing   anchoring

bounded rationality   marginal revenue and elasticity

ACTIVE REVIEW

Completion Questions

1. By understanding demand, a manager is learning about the ___customers___.

2. The responsiveness of consumers to changes in price is measure by ___elasticity___.

3. ___Price elasticity of demand___ measures the responsive of quantity demanded to changes in price.

4. Price elasticity of demand is the ratio of the ___% Δ in quantity demanded___ to the ___% Δ in price___.

5. When price elasticity of demand is greater than one, demand is said to be ___elastic___.

6. When price elasticity of demand is less than one, demand is said to be ___inelastic___.

7. When price elasticity of demand is equal to one, demand is said to be of ___unit elastic___.

8. A perfectly elastic demand curve is ___horizontal___.

9. A perfectly inelastic demand curve is ___vertical___.

10. Addictive drugs have a demand curve that is probably very ___inelastic___.

11. Once a specific elasticity number is known, changes in ___revenue___ can be determined from changes in price.

12. If demand is inelastic and price is increased, total revenue will ___increase___.

13. When demand is of unit elasticity, total revenue is ___constant___ regardless of whether price is increased or decreased.

14. If a manager recommends a price cut as a way to increase revenue, she must think that demand is ___elastic___.

15. ___Income elasticity of demand___ is used to measure the responsiveness of quantity demanded to changes in income.

16. Products with high income elasticities are often referred to as _Luxury goods_.

17. Normal goods are often called _cyclical goods_ and have income elasticities _> 0_.

18. Two goods may be classified as _substitutes_ or _complements_ based on the value of cross elasticity of demand.

19. Cross elasticity of demand is the ratio of the _% Δ in quant. demanded of a good_ to the _% Δ in price of another_.

20. Competitors should have cross elasticities that are _positive_.

21. The science of knowing the customer is called _revenue management_.

22. Firms often conduct _market research_ to learn about customers.

23. _Focus groups_ are a small number of consumers that are asked questions to determine buyer behavior.

24. _Secondary data_ is information collected for one purpose but used for another.

25. _Indifference curves_ is a graph that shows combinations of goods between which a consumer is indifferent.

26. If a consumer is indifferent between two combinations of goods, they are said to be _indifferent_ between them.

27. An indifference curve is downward sloping to show that consumers _substitute_ in order to remain indifferent between two goods.

28. Indifference curves are _downward sloping_ and cannot _cross_.

29. The combinations of goods that consumers can afford given their income and the prices of two goods is called the _budget line_.

30. The _marginal rate of substitution_ is the slope of an indifference curve.

31. Consumers often make choices by _framing_ and by _anchoring_.

True-False Questions

1. T (F)   Elasticity tells managers about the responsiveness of demand to change in price.

2. (T) F   Price elasticity tells managers something about moving along a demand curve when price changes.

3. T (F)   Elasticities are measured in absolute units.

4. (T) F   The more responsive consumers are to changes in price, the more elastic is their demand.

5. T F   If consumers are generally unresponsive to changes in price, then their demand is relatively inelastic.

6. T F   Elasticity is interpreted as a negative number.

7. T F   If the price elasticity of a product is .3, then for every one percent change in price there will be a 3 percent change in quantity demanded.

8. T F   A perfectly elastic demand curve is a vertical line.

9. T F   If demand is perfectly elastic, then a change in price will lead to a small change in quantity demanded.

10. T F   If price elasticity of demand is greater than one, demand is said to be elastic.

11. T F   Price elasticity of demand can be used to relate changes in revenue to changes in price.

12. T F   If price increases, total revenue may or may not change.

13. T F   In demand is inelastic, an increase in price will increase revenue but decrease quantity demanded.

14. T F   The lack of substitutes tends to make the demand for a product more elastic.

15. T F   In very short time periods, demand tends to be more elastic.

16. T F   Income elasticity may be used to determine if a product is a normal good or an inferior good.

17. T F   Inferior goods are also countercyclical goods.

18. T F   Income elasticity of demand is either greater than or less than one.

19. T F   Inferior goods may be determined by examining the cross elasticity of demand.

20. T F   In general, elasticity measures the responsiveness of one variable to changes in another.

21. T F   Substitute goods have positive cross elasticities of demand.

22. T F   If promotion elasticity is .008, then sales are very responsive to promotion activities.

23. T F   Substitutes and competitors are synonymous.

24. T F   Focus groups, surveys of buyers intentions and experiments are things businesses use to get to know the customer.

25. T F   Secondary data is applied to those things from which it was collected.

26. T F   Indifference analysis is a graphical way to demonstrate the law of demand.

27. T F   If a consumer is indifferent between two goods, then those two goods have equal marginal utilities.

28. T F   Indifference curves have positive slopes.

29. T F   A budget line shows all the combinations of two goods that a consumer can afford.

30. T F   Utility is maximized when the highest indifference curve is tangent to the budget line.

31. T F   Utility is minimized when a combination of goods is selected where the marginal rate of substitution is equal to the price ratio.

32. T F   The concept of framing is used to support the idea that consumers are rational in their choice behavior.

33. T F   When demand is elastic, marginal revenue is positive.

Multiple-Choice Questions

1. Demand curves tell managers that if they raise the price
   a. demand will fall.
   (b) quantity demanded will fall.
   c. revenue will rise.
   d. all of the above will occur.

2. The responsiveness of quantity demanded to changes in price is seen in
   a. cross elasticity of demand.
   b. income elasticity of demand.
   (c) price elasticity of demand.
   d. promotion elasticity.

3. When price elasticity is 1, demand is said to be
   (a) unit elastic.
   b. inelastic.
   c. elastic.
   d. none of the above.

4. When price elasticity is less than 1, demand is said to be
   a. unit elastic.
   (b) inelastic.
   c. elastic.
   d. none of the above.

5. When price elasticity is greater than 1, demand is said to be
   a. unit elastic.
   b. inelastic.
   (c) elastic.
   d. none of the above.

6. If demand is perfectly elastic, then a change in price
   a. will not affect quantity demanded.
   b. will reduce demand by good bit.
   c. will keep revenue constant.
   (d) will cause the quantity demanded to fall to zero.

7. If demand is perfectly inelastic, then the demand curve is
   a. horizontal.
   (b) vertical.
   c. downward sloping.
   d. a rectangular hyperbola.

8. If demand is perfectly inelastic, then a change in price
    a. will not affect quantity demanded.
    b. will reduce demand some.
    c. will keep revenue the same.
    d. will cause quantity demanded to fall to zero.

9. Addictive drugs probably have demand curves that are nearly
    a. perfectly elastic.
    b. unit elastic.
    c. perfectly inelastic.
    d. flat.

10. If total revenue rises as price rises, then
    a. demand is inelastic.
    b. demand is elastic.
    c. demand elasticity is unitary.
    d. demand elasticity cannot be determined.

11. If total revenue falls as price rises, then
    a. demand is inelastic.
    b. demand is elastic
    c. demand elasticity is unitary.
    d. demand elasticity cannot be determined.

12. If quantity demanded falls as price rises, then
    a. demand is inelastic.
    b. demand is elastic.
    c. demand elasticity is unitary.
    d. demand elasticity could be any of the above.

13. Price increases may cause total revenue to
    a. increase.
    b. decrease.
    c. remain constant.
    d. either a, b, or c.

14. The more substitutes a product has then
    a. the more inelastic will be its demand.
    b. the more elastic will be its demand.
    c. its demand will be unitary.
    d. none of the above.

15. Whether or not a product is inferior or normal can be determined by examining
    a. price elasticity of demand.
    b. cross elasticity of demand.
    c. income elasticity of demand.
    d. sales elasticity.

16. If the price of an inferior good rises, then its
    a. quantity demanded falls.
    b. quantity demanded rises.
    c. demand falls
    d. a and c are correct.

17. The income elasticity of normal goods is
    a. negative.
    (b.) positive.
    c. zero.
    d. the inverse of its cross elasticity.

18. If income increases and a product is cyclical, then
    a. quantity demanded rises.
    b. quantity demanded falls.
    (c.) demand increases.
    d. demand decreases.

19. Countercyclical goods are also
    a. normal goods.
    b. substitutes.
    c. complements.
    (d.) inferior goods.

20. Cross elasticity is the percentage change in the quantity demanded of one good
    (a.) resulting from a 1 percent change in the price of another good.
    b. resulting from a 1 percent change in its price.
    c. resulting from a 1 percent change in income.
    d. resulting from a 1 percent change in the promotion budget.

21. The cross elasticity of a complement is
    (a.) negative.
    b. zero.
    c. positive.
    d. the inverse of its income elasticity.

22. If two products produced by two different firms have a positive cross elasticity, then
    a. the products are substitutes.
    b. the products are complements.
    c. the firms are competitors.
    (d.) a and c are true.

23. Over long periods of time, demand tends to become more
    a. unit elastic.
    b. inelastic.
    (c.) elastic.
    d. vertical.

24. The science of knowing your customer is called
    a. economics.
    (b.) revenue management.
    c. statistics.
    d. buyer intentions.

25. Data that is collected for one purpose and used for another is called.
    a. primary data.
    b. focus group data.
    c. buyer intention data.
    (d.) secondary data

26. If a consumer is indifferent between two goods, then the two goods have the same
    a. marginal utility.
    b. average utility.
    c. total utility.
    d. dollar value

27. If two commodity bundles are on the same indifference curve, they have the same
    a. marginal utility.
    b. total utility
    c. average utility
    d. dollar value.

28. If two commodity bundles are on the same budget line, they have the same
    a. marginal utility.
    b. total utility.
    c. average utility.
    d. dollar value.

29. Using indifference analysis, the goal for the consumer is to find the commodity bundle
    a. that is on the highest indifference curve.
    b. that is on the lowest budget line.
    c. that is on the highest indifference curve for a given budget line.
    d. that is on the highest budget line for a given indifference curve.

30. When a consumer has maximized utility, the price ratio is equal to
    a. the marginal rate of substitution.
    b. marginal utility.
    c. total utility.
    d. the price elasticity of demand

31. When demand is elastic
    a. marginal revenue is negative.
    b. marginal revenue is positive.
    c. marginal revenue is zero.
    d. total revenue rises with price increases.

Short-Answer Questions

1. In general, what is the concept of elasticity trying to communicate?

2. What is the definition and the formula for price elasticity of demand?

3. What are the data requirements in order to calculate price elasticity of demand?

4. What does it mean if a demand curve is elastic?

5. What does it mean if a demand curve is inelastic?

6. Suppose you are told that increases in bus fares will bring increases in revenue but a decrease in ridership. How do you interpret this?

7. Assume that demand is perfectly inelastic but that the supply curve is upward sloping. What would happen to quantity demanded if there was a decrease in supply?

8. Why is a demand curve for a product more elastic when the product has many substitutes?

9. What does it mean if income elasticity of demand is positive?

10. Compare the meaning of income elasticity of demand and price elasticity of demand.

11. How might cross elasticity of demand be used to determine a business's competitors?

12. What happens to the quantity demanded when price is increased and demand is less than perfectly inelastic?

13. What are the sources of primary data?

14. What is secondary data?

15. What is an indifference curve?

16. Why does marginal utility vary along an indifference curve?

17. How does the budget line change when income changes?

18. How does the budget line change when a price changes?

19. What is the slope of an indifference curve?

20. Why were framing and anchoring developed?

Applications and Problems

1. A revenue management consultant tells you that she can increase your sales through focus group analysis and wishes to prepare a proposal for you to consider. She believes that she can create a marketing program based on this information that will increase your sales by $500,000 for this year and each of the next two. You need a bargaining plan if you wish to negotiate the consultant's fee. What is the most you would pay to hire this consultant? Your current cost of capital is 7 percent.

2. In the text it states that higher prices are associated with higher elasticities. According to this, if you have a downward sloping demand curve, then the upper portion of it (the part associated with high prices) should be elastic. What does revenue do as price falls over the entire range of the demand curve? Where is revenue maximized?

3. You have been asked to describe the possible effects of a government anti-drug policy of arresting crack cocaine dealers. The goal of the government is to reduce crack use. All you really know is that crack is addictive and that crack dealers probably want to make profits. What can you figure out about this plan using market analysis?

4. Why does a grocery store have the soft drinks near the potato chips? Why does it stock less chicken when it plans to have a sale on ground beef? Why does it put some salad dressing near the fresh lettuce?

5. Grocery stores often sell shelf space. They are very successful at getting high prices from the manufacturers of children's cereals for shelves that are 3.5 and 4.5 feet off the ground in the cereal section of the store. Why?

6. Assume that when the price of product a is $5, the quantity demanded is 10,000 units, and when the price falls to $4, the quantity demanded rises to 15,000 units. What is the price elasticity of demand? What will revenue do if price is reduced?

7. Who determines whether a product is normal or inferior or whether products are substitutes or complements and whether demand is elastic or inelastic? What do each of the formulas have in common?

Extending the Case Study: Knowing the Customer

Pricing decisions are not unlike advertising decisions. It is probably easy to see that the various forms of advertising are designed to affect sales in the different markets a business might find itself. Pricing does the same thing but most firms treat the pricing decision in a more haphazard or causal way. This makes little sense. From this and earlier chapters, you have seen that there is an inverse relationship between price and quantity demanded. Alternatively stated, the two variables that determine total revenue, price and quantity sold, move in opposite directions. Therefore, it becomes important to understand the magnitude of the movement of quantity when price changes. This is the purpose of elasticity. How responsive are your customers to changes in price? Are some of your customers more sensitive to price changes than others?

a. It is generally true that the passengers on a commercial airplane flight did not pay the same price for a ticket. Why would an airline charge different prices to customers depending on their date of purchase relative to the date of departure? Would it make sense in order to fill the plane to price the last seat at one dollar if that is what it took to fill it?

b. When would it pay to hire a consultant selling a revenue management system? Does the elasticity of demand affect your decision?

ANSWERS TO ACTIVE REVIEW QUESTIONS

Completion Questions

1. customers
2. elasticity
3. Price elasticity of demand
4. percentage change in the quantity demanded, percentage change in price
5. elastic
6. inelastic
7. unit elastic
8. horizontal
9. vertical
10. inelastic
11. revenue
12. increase
13. constant
14. elastic
15. Income elasticity of demand
16. luxury goods
17. cyclical goods, greater than zero
18. substitutes, complements

19. percentage change in the quantity demanded of a good, percentage change in the price of another.
20. positive
21. revenue management
22. market research
23. Focus groups
24. Secondary data
25. Indifference curves
26. indifferent
27. substitute
28. downward-sloping, cross
29. budget line
30. marginal rate of substitution
31. framing, anchoring

True-False Questions

1.	False	2.	True	3.	False
4.	True	5.	True	6.	False
7.	False	8.	False	9.	False
10.	True	11.	True	12.	True
13.	True	14.	False	15.	False
16.	True	17.	True	18.	False
19.	False	20.	True	21.	True
22.	False	23.	True	24.	True
25.	False	26.	True	27.	False
28.	False	29.	True	30.	True
31.	False	32.	False	33.	True

Multiple-Choice Questions

1.	b	2.	c	3.	a
4.	b	5.	c	6.	d
7.	b	8.	a	9.	c
10.	a	11.	b	12.	d
13.	d	14.	b	15.	c
16.	a	17.	b	18.	c
19.	d	20.	a	21.	a

22.	d	23.	c	24.	b
25.	d	26.	c	27.	b
28.	d	29.	c	30.	a
31.	b				

Short-Answer Questions

1. Elasticity attempts to communicate the responsiveness of one variable to changes in another.
2. The definition of price elasticity of demand is the percentage change in quantity demanded resulting from a one percent change in price. From this definition, price elasticity of demand is the percentage change in quantity demanded divided by the percentage change in price. This ratio is then multiplied by a negative one to make it positive.
3. To calculate price elasticity of demand you need to know two prices and their associated quantities. You need data off of a demand curve that is not shifting.
4. It means that the price elasticity of demand is greater than one. This is to say, the percentage change in the quantity demanded is greater than the percentage change in price.
5. It means that the price elasticity of demand is less than one. This is to say, the percentage change in the quantity demanded is less than the percentage change in price.
6. Apparently, the demand for bus service is inelastic. Raising fares will reduce the quantity demanded (the number of riders). However, the percentage decrease in quantity demanded is less than the percentage increase in price. As such, revenue will rise even with less riders.
7. A perfectly inelastic demand curve is vertical. Quantity demanded is the same regardless of the price. Therefore, a decrease is supply (a leftward shift) would cause price to rise and quantity demanded will be unaffected.
8. The first response of consumers when the price of a product rises is to look for a substitute. If many are available, then it is easy to replace one product of another. Therefore, demand would be more elastic.
9. Income elasticity is defined as the percentage change in the quantity demanded of a product divided by the percentage change in income. If this ratio is positive, it means that income and quantity demanded move in the same direction. This is the definition of a normal good.
10. Price elasticity of demand measures the responsiveness of quantity demanded to changes in price. It is telling you what happens when you move along a demand curve. Income elasticity of demand measures the responsiveness of quantity demanded when income changes. It is telling you how the demand curve shifts when income changes
11. Another word for competitors is substitutes. Cross elasticity is used to identify how the quantity demanded of one good responds to the price changes of another. Therefore, cross elasticity of demand can identify substitute goods.
12. Quantity demanded falls. Elasticity tells you the extent of its movement. It still falls however.
13. Primary data can come from things like focus groups, surveys, buyer intention analysis and experiments.
14. Secondary data is data that have been collected for one purpose but is used for another.
15. An indifference curve is a set of commodity bundles that have the same total utility.
16. The marginal utility of a product depends on the amount of that product you already have. As you move along an indifference curve, the number of units of each product in the commodity bundle changes. Therefore, the marginal utility of each product changes.

17. The budget line will shift parallel to itself. If income increases it will shift outward while a decrease in income will cause the budget line to shift inward.
18. The slope of the budget line will change whenever there is a change in a price of one of the two products. The exception to this is if the prices change in the same direction and in the same proportion.
19. The slope of an indifference curve is the marginal rate of substitution.
20. Framing and anchoring are attempts to explain consumer choice without totally relying on an assumption of rationality.

Applications and Problems

1. The consultant can increase your sales by $500,000 per year for this year and the next two. You must discount the future benefits in order to get their value today. The appropriate rate of discount is your cost of capital. The present value of the additional sales is $500,000 + ($500,000/1.07) + ($500,000/(1.07)^2) = $1,405,885. This benefit sets the upper limit to what you would be willing to pay.
2. The upper portion of a downward sloping demand curve is elastic. When demand is elastic, revenue rises as prices fall. So, at first, revenue will rise as you move down the demand curve by lowering price. However, as you move down the demand curve, elasticity falls. Eventually you will get to a point where the elasticity changes from elastic to inelastic and further price cuts will lead to declines in revenue. So, at first revenue rose and then it fell. It is maximized at the point where elasticity switches from being greater than one to being less than one. This is the point of unit elasticity.
3. If crack is addictive, it is safe to assume that its demand is perfectly inelastic – demand is vertical. It is also safe to assume that dealers would bring more to the market as the price goes up – the supply curve is upward sloping to the right. Taking some dealers off the market would shift the supply curve to the left. As a result, the price on the street would rise. The important point is that this does nothing to demand. The result of the policy is to cause the price to rise. The perfect inelasticity of the demand curve assures you that the quantity demanded will not be affected by the increase in price, however. Also, due to the nature of the demand curve, the revenue of the remaining crack dealers will go up – and possibly their profits.
4. It does these things as part of its marketing campaign. Soft drinks and potato chips, and lettuce and salad dressing exhibit a complementary relationship. So, store managers feel that when people are buying soft drinks they may be also inclined to buy potato chips if they are handy to the drinks. The beef and chicken case deals with substitutes. Store managers must feel that the lower price of ground beef will promote its purchase, but at the expense of chicken purchases. This is simply getting to know the customer.
5. This is another example of getting to know the customer. Marketing studies show that the primary decision maker in a cereal purchase is the child. As such, manufacturers want their product at the eye level of children. Demand for this space is intense and, thereby, very inelastic.
6. Substitute the data into the formula. ((15,000-10,000)/10,000) /((4-5)/5) = -2.50*(-1)=2.5. Demand is elastic. As a result, a cut in price will lead to an increase in revenue.
7. The common element in all the formulas is the change in quantity demanded. The formulas differ by what causes the change in the quantity demanded. Consumers determine the responsiveness of quantity demanded to changes in the price of a product, changes in income, or changes in the price of some other good. So in each of the formulas, we find the consumer.

ANSWERS TO CASE STUDY QUESTIONS

Extending the Case Study: Knowing the Customer

a. The date of purchase relative to the date of departure may indicate different price elasticities of demand among the customers. People shopping for tickets a few weeks a way from the date of departure have more time to shop among all the alternative ways to get to a given destination. Late ticket buyers have little search time. Time affects a consumers' knowledge of substitutes and, thereby, affects the price elasticity of demand. So, instead of charging everyone the same price, airlines find that revenue is increased if they charge late buyers more and early buyers less. Ticket purchases on or near the date of departure may indicate a more inelastic demand compared to travelers that shop around for awhile. The airline may sell more tickets to them and increase revenue by charging a lower price as they may have a more elastic demand for air travel.

b. Does it make sense to charge just one dollar at the last moment to sell the last seat? Yes. The additional costs to the airline of the last passenger are probably zero. The plane is about the leave anyway. So, the one dollar directly goes to profit. It would pay to hire the consultant if their contribution to revenue from providing additional information exceeds their costs. Elasticity probably has little to do with the decision. If demand is elastic, price increases will decrease revenue. A consultant might help us understand this. At the same time, if demand is inelastic, we need to know how high we can increase our price to get the greatest affect on revenue.

CHAPTER 5

Costs

CHAPTER OVERVIEW

The goal of business should be to maximize economic profits – to add value. As stated earlier this is the difference between revenue and all costs of production including the costs of capital. In Chapter 4 we focused on the inseparable items of revenue and knowing the customer. In Chapter 5 the costs of production are examined.

　　The place a discussion of costs must begin is not with costs themselves. The discussion must start with the actual physical process of turning inputs into outputs. Central to this conversion is the law of diminishing marginal returns. This law describes the relationship between changes in variable inputs and the resulting change in output given that some inputs are fixed. At first the marginal returns from adding variable inputs rises rapidly and then more slowly. From this law it is a simple leap to begin to understand why the costs of production behave in the way they do over the short run and over the long run. Within the study of costs the topics of economies and diseconomies of scale and economies of scope can been developed. Chapter 5 concludes by putting into an economic context business jargon like the experience curve, downsizing, outsourcing, joint venture, and supply chain management.

　　One of the most important relationships developed in this chapter is the relationship between marginal product and marginal costs. In fact, marginal cost is derived from marginal product. The appendix formally presents its derivation.

KEY CONCEPTS FOR REVIEW

short run	long run
law of diminishing returns	average total costs (ATC)
marginal costs (MC)	average variable costs (AVC)
total costs (TC)	total variable costs (TVC)
total fixed costs (TFC)	short run average total costs (SRATC)
long run average total costs (LRATC)	economies of scale
diseconomies of scale	economies of scope
constant returns to scale	outsourcing
downsizing	joint ventures
supply chain	variable inputs
fixed inputs	overhead costs
direct costs	

ACTIVE REVIEW

Completion Questions

1. To understand profit, managers must not only know the customer, they must also understand _____costs_____.

2. At times, managers focused on cost lose sight of the fact that their goal should be to _____add value_____.

3. To begin to understand costs, one must first begin to understand _____production_____.

4. The _____short run_____ is a period of time during which at least one input is fixed.

5. When all inputs are variable, a business is in the _____long run_____.

6. The short-run relationship between inputs and outputs is called the _____law of diminishing marginal returns_____.

7. According to the law of diminishing marginal returns, as units of a variable are added to the production process, at first total output increases _____rapidly_____ and then more _____slowly_____.

8. Production always takes place in the _____short run_____.

9. In accounting, cost are often classified as being either _____overhead_____ or _____direct_____.

10. Economists classify costs as being either _____fixed_____ or _____variable_____.

11. Due to the law of diminishing returns, initially _____total output_____ rises more rapidly than _____total cost_____.

12. _____Average total costs_____ is determined by dividing total costs by total output.

13. _____Marginal cost_____ is the change in total costs that comes from producing another unit of output.

14. If ATC is rising, then MC must be _____greater_____ than ATC.

15. Variable costs depend upon the _____volume of production_____.

16. _____Fixed costs_____ do not change with the _____volume of production_____.

17. Total costs are the sum of _____variable costs_____ and _____fixed costs_____.

18. Average total costs are the sum of _____average variable costs_____ and _____avg. fixed costs_____.

19. ATC and AVC may be described as _____U-shaped_____.

20. MC passes through the _____minimum_____ of ATC and AVC.

21. The long run is often called the _____planning horizon_____.

22. In the short run, mangers can decided on how much of a _variable input_ they employ but in the long run they can also decide on how much of a _fixed input_ they should use.

23. When managers change the amount of a capital resource to use, the _SRATC curve_ shifts.

24. The _LRATC curve_ traces out the pattern formed by many _SRATC curves_.

25. If, in the long run, unit costs decrease as production increases, we say there are _economics of scale_.

26. If, in the long run, unit costs increase as production increases, we say there are _diseconomics of scale_.

27. If, in the long run, unit costs remain constant as production increases, we say there are _constant returns to scale_.

28. Size does not automatically improve _efficiently_.

29. If a long-run average cost curve is u-shaped, then it exhibits _economics of scale_, _diseconomics of scale_, and _constant returns to scale_.

30. There is some evidence that economies of scale may explain the patterns of _trade_ between countries.

31. _Economics of scope_ occur when a company obtains a production advantage from producing more than one product.

32. Economies of scale are often confused with the _experience of learning curve_.

33. _Downsizing_ may be described as moving to a different short-run average total cost curve.

34. After downsizing, accounting cost will _rise_ unless there is an increase in _efficiency_.

35. _Outsourcing_ is purchasing services outside a company that used to be produced inside the company.

36. _Supply chain mgmt_ refers to attempts to reduce costs at each or any given step in the _supply chain_.

True-False Questions

1. (T) F   To understand costs managers must first understand production.

2. T (F)   The goal of managers is to minimize costs.

3. T (F)   At first, when variable inputs are added to fixed inputs, total production increases ~~slowly~~ quickly.

4. (T) F   New variable inputs create additional costs and additional revenues.

5. (T) F   At first, when variable inputs are added to fixed inputs, total production increases rapidly.

6. T (F)   There are no variable inputs in the short run.

7. T (F)   Even in the long run, there are ~~a few fixed inputs.~~ *all variable inputs*

8. (T) F   The law of diminishing returns applies only in the short run.

9. (T) F   According to the law of diminishing marginal returns, eventually each additional air bag will add little additional benefit.

10. T (F)   Managers need to understand costs before they can understand production. *production* *costs*

11. (T) F   Initially, total output rises more rapidly than total costs.

12. T (F)   If marginal costs are greater than average total costs, then average total costs will fall with additional production.

13. T (F)   ATC is defined as total ~~output multiplied by total costs.~~ *costs divided by total output*

14. T (F)   Economist classify costs as being either ~~overhead or direct.~~ *variable or fixed*

15. (T) F   Total costs are the sum of total variable costs and total fixed costs.

16. T (F)   Average fixed costs are a constant.

17. (T) F   Marginal costs cut through the lowest point of average variable costs and average total costs.

18. T (F)   Marginal costs are related to average fixed costs.

19. (T) F   Marginal costs describe how variable costs change with additional output.

20. (T) F   The long run and the planning horizon are synonymous.

21. (T) F   In the long run, fixed inputs become variable.

22. T (F)   As capital resources are added, the long-run average cost curves shifts.

23. (T) F   Long run average cost curves trace out the pattern of shifting short run average costs curves.

24. (T) F   Economies of scale are present if the long run average cost curve is downward sloping.

25. (T) F   The long run average costs curve show the lowest average costs when all inputs are variable.

26. T (F)   Constant returns to scale are seen as an upward sloping, long run average cost curve.

27. T (F)   Size and efficiency are perfectly related.

28. T (F)   The existence of economies of scale means that managers need to plan to make their company very big.

29. (T) F   Often, size requires specialized management.

30. (T) F   Firms should consider market demand when making the decision to expand capital resources.

31. T (F)   Economies of scope is another way to describe economies of scale.

32. T (F)   Economies of scope is the foundation of the learning curve.

33. (T) F   Economies of scope occur when the costs of producing multiple products jointly is less than the costs of producing them separately.

34. (T) F   The learning curve can be confused sometimes with increases in technology.

35. T (F)   Downsizing is the rationale often used to justify corporate expansion.

36. (T) F   Outsourcing is based on the idea that someone else can produce something cheaper than you can.

37. (T) F   Economies of scale may be used to understand why countries trade what the do.

38. (T) F   Access to markets is a reason for a joint venture.

39. T (F)   To attain economies of scale, a company should produce along the entire supply chain.

Multiple-Choice Questions

1. To understand profits, managers must understand
   a. revenue and demand.
   b. costs and production.
   (c.) revenue and costs.
   d. sales and demand elasticity.

2. The goal of managers should be to
   a. maximize sales.
   (b.) add value.
   c. minimize costs.
   d. increase market share.

3. To understand costs a manager must
   a. understand demand.
   b. understand profit.
   c. the market prices of inputs.
   (d.) production.

4. The relationship between inputs and outputs is seen in
   (a.) the law of diminishing marginal returns.
   b. the law of diminishing marginal utility.
   c. the law of demand.
   d. both a and b.

5. The law of diminishing marginal returns states that when variable inputs are first added to fixed inputs, production increases
   a. slowly.
   b. at a constant rate.
   (c.) rapidly.
   d. slowly and then rapidly.

6. The period of time over which there is a least one fixed input, is the
    a. long run.
    b. short run.
    c. the learning period
    d. planning horizon.

7. Over the long run
    a. all inputs are variable.
    b. most inputs are variable.
    c. average costs fall.
    d. only capital inputs are variable.

8. According to the law of diminishing marginal returns it is possible that by adding variable inputs to fixed inputs
    a. total output will grow.
    b. total output will not change.
    c. total output will fall.
    d. all are possible.

9. If marginal returns are rising rapidly
    a. marginal costs will rise.
    b. marginal costs will fall.
    c. marginal costs will remain constant.
    d. average total costs will rise.

10. Marginal cost cuts average total cost
    a. at the low point of marginal costs.
    b. anywhere along the downward sloping portion.
    c. at the minimum of ATC.
    d. at the minimum of AVC.

11. Economists classify costs as being either
    a. overhead or direct.
    b. fixed or direct.
    c. variable or fixed.
    d. overhead or variable.

12. If average variable costs are falling,
    a. marginal costs must be less than average variable costs.
    b. marginal costs must be rising.
    c. marginal cost is at a minimum.
    d. fixed costs have been minimized.

13. Average fixed costs equal
    a. total costs minus total variable costs.
    b. average total costs plus average variable costs.
    c. marginal costs divided by output.
    d. total fixed costs divided by output.

14. Marginal costs represent
    a. the change in total costs when a variable input is added.
    b. the change in total costs when another unit of output is produced.
    c. the change in average total costs when output is changed.
    d. none of the above.

15. The planning horizon is similar to the
    a. short run.
    b. long run.
    c. learning period.
    d. market period.

16. In the planning period
    a. all inputs are variable.
    b. most inputs are fixed.
    c. only one input is fixed.
    d. capital resources are fixed.

17. In the planning horizon
    a. variable inputs are constant.
    b. new capital can be added, but no new firms may enter the market.
    c. economists examine only accounting costs.
    d. fixed inputs can be changed.

18. The long run average cost curve traces out
    a. short run marginal costs curves.
    b. short run average variable cost curves.
    c. short run average total cost curves.
    d. short run learning curves.

19. When capital resources are changed
    a. the long run average cost curves shifts.
    b. marginal cost is unaffected.
    c. the short run average total cost curve shifts.
    d. total fixed costs decrease.

20. Economies of scale occur when
    a. long run average costs fall.
    b. long run average costs rise.
    c. long run average cost stay constant.
    d. long run average costs shift.

21. Diseconomies of scale occur when
    a. long run average costs fall.
    b. long run average costs rise.
    c. long run average cost stay constant.
    d. long run average costs shift.

22. Constant returns to scale occur when
    a. long run average costs fall.
    b. long run average costs rise.
    c. long run average cost stay constant.
    d. long run average costs shift.

23. Specialization is limited by the size
    a. of capital inputs.
    b. of the short run.
    c. of economies of scale.
    d. of the market.

24. When the costs of producing several products jointly is cheaper than producing them separately,
    a. there are economies of scale.
    b. there is a learning curve.
    (c.) there are economies of scope.
    d. there are diseconomies of scope.

25. When firms move to a different short run average total cost curve,
    a. the are outsourcing.
    (b.) they are downsizing.
    c. they ignore joint ventures.
    d. they are moving along their experience curve.

26. If a college allows a hotel company to run its dorms, it is
    (a.) outsourcing.
    b. downsizing.
    c. doing a joint venture.
    d. worried over its supply chain.

27. Often, companies that want to enter a foreign market
    a. downsize.
    (b.) look for a joint venture.
    c. outsource.
    d. manage the supply chain.

Short-Answer Questions

1. Why does a manager need to understand production in order to understand costs?

2. Is studying costs the same things as studying how managers add value?

3. Does the law of diminishing marginal returns exist in the long run?

4. What is the law of diminishing marginal returns?

5. Are the number of air bags used in a car subject to the law of diminishing marginal returns?

6. How does the law of diminishing marginal returns connect to the costs of production?

7. How do accountants and economists classify costs?

8. Describe the relationship between marginal costs and average costs but use a baseball player's batting average for the season and for one game as the context.

9. What is the nature of the long run?

10. How is the long run depicted?

11. What does the long run average cost curve show?

12. What do short run average total costs do when fixed resources change?

13. When do economies of scale occur?

14. When do diseconomies of scale occur?

15. Why is the long run average cost curve U-shaped?

16. Is it possible for a company to be too big?

17. Why might an experience curve be confused with economies of scale?

18. Why might an business downsize or outsource?

19. Define marginal product in terms of calculus.

20. Define marginal cost in terms of calculus.

Applications and Problems

1. Assume that you are in charge of making the decision to outsource the business office of a hospital that you manage. How would you make the decision?

2. Given what you determined in Question 1, how might an outsourcing company get you to pay more than the amount you determined.

3. Assume your cost function is C = $15,000 + $8000Q. Without numbers for Q, describe the calculation of TC, TVC, TFC, ATC, AVC, AFC, and MC.

4. What is unusual about MC in the above problem? Why?

5. Assume you can dispose of waste by either bagging it up and paying someone to carry it off to the landfill or pumping it into a creek and letting it flow downstream. Which would you do to minimize costs? What do you end up doing? What would happen if you had to pay a price to use the creek to carry away your waste?

6. Could management methods contribute to diseconomies of scale?

7. Assume you start an internet company. You build your web site and start to advertise for business. What problem do you immediately have that new businesses started in the pre-internet years did not.

8. Often when downsizing is discussed, only costs are mentioned. Discuss downsizing in terms of profits.

Extending the Case Study: Mrs. Fields' Cookies

The case clearly shows the relationship between size, costs, and production. It may seem obvious to some, but others act as if they have little knowledge of these linkages. Production decisions and the behavior of costs are simply two sides of the same coin. Decisions that determine the process of physically changing inputs into goods and services dictate, to a very large degree, the way costs will behave as output changes. As a firm grows, the marginal returns to output of adding variables inputs slows, thereby causing marginal costs of additional output to rise. If market opportunities are there to support further expansion, managers must decide whether or not to expand their fixed inputs. As part of this, managers must be open to the possibility that there are better ways to convert inputs, both fixed and variable, into output. The identification of goods and services that customers value is not the only part of adding value. Managers must always examine processes that convert inputs into outputs.

a. How did inertia play a role in the demise of Mrs. Fields' Cookies?

b. What are some ways to overcome inertia in decision making?

c. What may have the managers of Mrs. Fields' Cookies lost sight of?

ANSWERS TO ACTIVE REVIEW QUESTIONS

Completion Questions

1. costs
2. add value
3. production
4. short run
5. long run
6. law of diminishing marginal returns
7. rapidly, slowly
8. short run
9. overhead, direct
10. fixed, variable
11. total output, total costs
12. Average total costs
13. Marginal cost
14. greater
15. volume of production
16. Fixed costs, volume of production
17. variable costs, fixed costs
18. average variable costs, average fixed costs
19. u-shaped
20. minimum
21. planning horizon
22. variable input, fixed input
23. short run average total cost curve
24. long run average cost curve, short run average total cost curves
25. economies of scale
26. diseconomies of scale
27. constant returns to scale
28. efficiency
29. economies of scale, diseconomies of scale, constant returns to scale
30. trade
31. economies of scope
32. experience or learning curve
33. Downsizing
34. rise, efficiency
35. Outsourcing

36. Supply chain management, supply chain

True-False Questions

1.	True	2.	False	3.	False
4.	True	5.	True	6.	False
7.	False	8.	True	9.	True
10.	False	11.	True	12.	False
13.	False	14.	False	15.	True
16.	False	17.	True	18.	False
19.	True	20.	True	21.	True
22.	False	23.	True	24.	True
25.	True	26.	False	27.	False
28.	False	29.	True	30.	True
31.	False	32.	False	33.	True
34.	True	35.	False	36.	True
37.	True	38.	True	39.	False

Multiple-Choice Questions

1.	c	2.	b	3.	d
4.	a	5.	c	6.	b
7.	a	8.	d	9.	b
10.	c	11.	c	12.	a
13.	d	14.	b	15.	b
16.	a	17.	d	18.	c
19.	c	20.	a	21.	b
22.	c	23.	d	24.	c
25.	b	26.	a	27.	b

Short-Answer Questions

1. The costs of production represent expenditures on inputs. The employment of inputs depends upon what the manager knows about transforming inputs into output. So, a given level of employment of inputs and how they are arranged determines the expenditures on inputs or the costs of production.

2. No. Adding value is the same thing as earning economic profits. Economic profits are the difference between revenue and the costs of production including the cost of capital. Therefore, studying costs is only one part of the study of adding value.

3. No. The law of diminishing marginal returns describes what happens to output when variable inputs are added to fixed inputs. The long run is a period of time over which there are no fixed inputs. It is a planning horizon. All production occurs in the presence of fixed inputs, so all production is subject to the law of diminishing marginal returns and occurs in the short run.

4. The law of diminishing marginal returns describes the relationship between variable inputs and output in the short run. As variable inputs are added to fixed inputs, total output grows, at first rapidly and then slowly.

5. One might expect the first air bag to give the greatest benefit if it is used to protect the driver. The second air bag adds benefits only if there is a front seat passenger. Other air bags, while adding safety, contribute less.

6. Assume that you know the per-unit price of the variable input. As the variable input is added to a fixed input, initially total output rises more rapidly than costs, and then, after some point, costs begin to rise more rapidly than output. As such, average total costs would fall initially and then begin to rise.

7. Accountants classify costs as either overhead or as direct costs. Economists describe costs as either fixed or variable. The classification is based on the ability to change them during the short run. Fixed costs cannot be changed in the short run and are, therefore, independent of output. Variable costs change with changes in production.

8. Averages rise when the marginal is above the average and fall when reversed. A baseball player's batting average is based on all the at-bats up to a given game. The next game – the marginal game – is added to the average. So, if for the season, the player is batting .200 and goes 4 for 4 in the next game – bats 1.000 – then when the marginal game is added to all the other games, the season's average will rise. If they fail to get a hit, the average will fall. This is the same thing as saying if the marginal unit of output costs more to produce than the average of all the others, then when it is added to all the others, the average will rise.

9. The long run is a period of time over which all inputs can be varied. This includes capital resources as well.

10. The long run is shown by the long run average cost curve. The long run average cost curve is tangent to or just touches each short run average cost curve.

11. The long run average cost curve shows the lowest per-unit cost of output for every level of output when all resources are variable.

12. Short run average total cost curves are built on the assumption that there is at least one fixed input. So, when the fixed input changes, the short run average total cost curve will shift.

13. Economies of scale occur when the per-unit costs of production decrease when output increases, given that all resources are variable.

14. Diseconomies of scale occur when the per-unit costs of production increase when output increases, given that all resources are variable.

15. A U-shaped long run average cost curve is exhibiting all types of returns to scale. When it is downward sloping there are economies of scale, and when it is upward sloping there are diseconomies of scale. Constant returns to scale cover the flat region.

16. Yes. If businesses get big simply to take advantage of economies of scale, they may be making a mistake. A business's size is determined in large part by the size of the market it serves.

17. A downward sloping experience curve is based on the idea that the more you do something, the better you will become. As such, per-unit costs should fall. While this is true, it is also true that average costs may fall with new technology holding your knowledge constant.

18. Downsizing or outsourcing may be of interest to managers if they learn that they can add value by rearranging the structure of the production process. In outsourcing, an external company produces something cheaper compared to the originating company. In downsizing, the business moves to another short run average total cost curve.
19. Marginal product is the partial derivative of the production function with respect to changes in labor.
20. Marginal cost is the partial derivative of the total cost function with respect to changes in output.

Applications and Problems

1. A very simple way might be to collect data on what you now spend to run the business office. From past data you may also build an expected growth rate for future expenses. Next, determine how many years you might want the outsourcing contract to cover. Given this information you can calculate the present value (discounting at the cost of capital) of your anticipated business office expenditures. If the outsourcing company offers to run the business office for more than this amount, it makes sense for you to continue doing it yourself.

2. It is often the case that outsourcing companies sell their services for more than the present value of internal expenses. They argue that by outsourcing one function to them, their presence will make the other functions you continue to run more efficient. For example, with a better business office, your admitting function can be made more efficient. The outsourcing company may also argue that you are underestimating the future costs. These extra benefits will be built into their bid.

3. TC: the cost function itself gives total cost. All you need is Q. TFC: these are costs that don't change with output. This is seen in the $15,000. TVC: These are the costs that depend on output. Thus, TVC = $8000Q. ATC = ($15,000 + $8000Q)/Q. AFC = $15,000/Q. AVC = ($8000Q)/Q. Marginal costs are the change in costs when output changes. If Q changes by one, costs change by $8000. So MC = $8000.

4. Marginal cost is constant. Given the existence of the law of diminishing marginal utility, marginal costs should, at first, fall and then rise.

5. It may well be the case that it is cheaper to pump it into the creek. Once you build the pump, the creek does the rest. You end up being a polluter if the waste harms others downstream. If there is a charge to use the creek, it may start to pay to haul the waste to the landfill. Economists argue that pollution occurs because resources are used but not paid for.

6. Diseconomies of scale occur when the long run average cost curve starts to slope upward to the right. As you move up the long run average cost curve, a business is getting bigger and bigger. As such, all the human relationships that must be managed get more and more numerous and more and more complicated. These complications are one of the many things that makes efficiency difficult to maintain in large businesses.

7. The internet will allow your company to have access to worldwide business. You will have to deal with the possibility of being big right away. In the pre-internet world, the problem of market size was not really an issue. Internet companies have had to learn to be big immediately.

8. It is true that downsizing reduces costs in the short term. It is also true, that if a firm has fewer inputs, it will have less output unless new efficiencies can be identified. So,

downsizing reduces costs and revenue. The resulting impact on profits will be determined by the relative size of the declines in both costs and revenue.

ANSWERS TO CASE STUDY QUESTIONS

Extending the Case Study: Mrs. Fields' Cookies

a. From the case it is obvious that the Fields' insistence on maintaining the original production process that stressed a high degree of centralization was a source of their failure. It very well may have been the case that there was a feeling that the way they always had done things was the source of their success. It seems reasonable for people to want to continue to be successful. As such, it also seems reasonable that they would want to maintain the production process and control that they thought was part of their success. The problem was that this structure was inappropriate as the company expanded. They thought their success was the way they made things rather than recognizing that they had succeeded because they had added value.

b. External consultants may help overcome internal inertia. Firms external to a company find profit opportunities in identifying places of cost savings or new sources of efficiency in other companies. By seeking profit, these firms have it in their interest to maximize savings that are possible from a new arrangement of production activities. Another source for overcoming inertia is the stock market. The stock market is pricing shares that represent claims on profits. As discussed in Chapter 2, the market is actually pricing the present value of future economic profits. If stock price suffers, this suggests that the market sees a decline in future added value. This may motivate management to reconsider things that, at the time, appear to be sacred cows. Management incentive schemes related to stock performance may also discourage inertia.

c. They may have lost sight of the fact that the goal of business is to add value rather than maintain the status quo.

CHAPTER 6

Profit Maximization: Seeking Competitive Advantage

CHAPTER OVERVIEW

We have seen over the previous chapters that the primary economic goal of managers is to maximize added value. Within this context several important issues have been explored. First, the concept of economic profit was revealed. Next, the importance of knowing the customer was connected to revenue. Most recently, the connection between inputs, outputs, and costs was initiated with a discussion of the law of diminishing marginal returns.

In order to beginning examining how managers add value, we must identify some rule that guides decision making. To this end, the present chapter begins with a discussion of profit maximization or the MR=MC rule. Economists apply this rule to all types of decisions. In deciding whether or not to do something, you should always consider the additional revenue or benefit (MR) that will result from your decision and compare that to the additional costs associated with your decision. If MR is greater than MC, you should do more of whatever it is you are doing.

The next part of Chapter 6 describes the various types of environments in which business decisions are made. These environments, or markets, range from perfect competition to monopoly on the extremes to monopolistic competition and oligopoly in between. It is in these selling markets that managers attempt to create and maintain economic profit over time.

The chapter concludes with an appendix that formally develops the rules for profit maximization for both price takers and price makers. A calculus-based framework is employed.

KEY CONCEPTS FOR REVIEW

profit maximization	marginal revenue
marginal cost	MR=MC rule
differentiated products	standardized products
price taker	perfect competition
monopoly	monopolistic competition
oligopoly	strategic behavior
kinked demand curve	prisoner's dilemma
sustained competitive advantage	barriers to entry
present value	market structures

ACTIVE REVIEW

Completion Questions

1. The objective of business is to create _____.

2. The rule of profit maximization states that marginal revenue minus marginal cost should equal _____.

3. _____ is the additional revenue obtained by selling one more unit of output.

4. If marginal revenue of the last unit is greater than the marginal cost of that unit, the output should _____.

5. Every decision faced by a manager can be placed within the _____.

6. The next unit should not be produced if its _____ is greater than its _____.

7. While the calculation of marginal revenue and marginal cost may be difficult, the rule of profit maximization still provides a _____ for decision making.

8. The selling environment may also be described as the _____ for a firm's output.

9. Market structures include _____, _____, _____, and _____.

10. In a competitive market, each firm is a _____.

11. In a competitive market a _____ can only sell at the _____.

12. A firm in a competitive market does not have a _____ to keep others out.

13. A firm in a competitive market faces a _____ demand curve.

14. A market with a single seller is called a _____.

15. A monopoly has the ability to _____.

16. Monopolies can arise when there are large _____ in production.

17. _____ is the main feature of monopolistic competition.

18. When there is easy entry into a market, firms find it difficult to maintain _____.

19. In an _____, firms often engage in _____.

20. If what I do depends on what you do, then I might engage in _____.

21. The _____ and _____ are examples of strategic behavior.

22. To sustain a competitive advantage, a firm must often create a _____.

23. The value today of an amount that will be paid or received in the future is called the _____.

24. Calculating a present value is called _____.

25. The further away a payment is to be received, the _____ will be its present value.

True-False Questions

1. T F   The goal of managers should be to maximize added value.

2. T F   Profits have been maximized when the difference between marginal revenue and marginal cost is the greatest.

3. T F   Profits have been maximized when the difference between marginal revenue and marginal cost is zero.

4. T F   Total output multiplied by the market price is equal to marginal revenue.

5. T F   Marginal costs is the change in total fixed costs when additional output is produced.

6. T F   You should do more of something if marginal revenue is greater than marginal costs.

7. T F   You should do less of something if marginal revenue is less than marginal costs.

8. T F   When profits have been maximized, economic profit is always the greatest.

9. T F   Calculating marginal revenue and marginal cost is pretty straightforward.

10. T F   Entry is easy in perfect competition.

11. T F   Each firm in perfect competition is a price maker.

12. T F   A price taker cannot affect the market price by changing production.

13. T F   A price taker faces a perfectly inelastic demand curve.

14. T F   A monopoly is a single seller.

15. T F   Monopolies have a barrier to entry.

16. T F   Large economies of scale can lead to a monopoly.

17. T F   Monopolies are price makers.

18. T F   A firm in perfect competition tries to differentiate its product.

19. T F   A firm in monopolistic competition is not a price taker.

20. T   F   A firm in monopolistic competition can block entry.

21. T   F   It is difficult to enter an oligopolistic market.

22. T   F   Strategic behavior occurs in an oligopoly.

23. T   F   The kinked demand curve is based on the idea that price decisions by one firm is partially dependent on the pricing decisions of others.

24. T   F   A prisoner's dilemma is found in monopoly.

25. T   F   If my behavior is dependent on what you do, then our actions are independent.

26. T   F   Barriers of entry are needed to sustain a competitive advantage.

27. T   F   A present value is the current value of a payment or a cost that will be received or paid in the future.

Multiple-Choice Questions

1. The goals of mangers should be to maximize
   a. market share.
   b. sales.
   c. economic profit.
   d. employee satisfaction.

2. According to the rule of profit maximization, output should continue to expand as long as
   a. marginal revenue is less than marginal cost.
   b. marginal revenue is greater than marginal cost.
   c. marginal revenue is equal to marginal cost.
   d. marginal revenue is equal to the market price.

3. According to the rule of profit maximization, output should be reduced if
   a. marginal revenue is less than marginal cost.
   b. marginal revenue is greater than marginal cost.
   c. marginal revenue is equal to marginal cost.
   d. marginal revenue is equal to the market price.

4. Profits have been maximized if
   a. marginal revenue is less than marginal cost.
   b. marginal revenue is greater than marginal cost.
   c. marginal revenue is equal to marginal cost.
   d. marginal revenue is equal to the market price.

5. Marginal revenue and marginal cost can be calculated in the real world
   a. easily.
   b. if accounting rules are used appropriately.
   c. only if the market is competitive.
   d. with difficulty.

6. In a competitive market each firm is a
   a. price maker.
   b. price taker.
   c. market maker.
   d. profit maker.

7. Over the long run, firms in a competitive market
   a. cannot earn economic profits.
   b. can earn economic profits.
   c. can add value.
   d. earn profit beyond the cost of capital.

8. Entry
   a. increases economic profit in the short run.
   b. increases normal profit in the long run.
   c. reduces economic profits to zero over the long run.
   d. decreases normal profit in the long run.

9. A market with a single seller
   a. is a monopoly.
   b. is an oligopoly.
   c. exhibits product differentiation.
   d. is competitive.

10. Monopolies can come into existence
    a. with patents.
    b. with government grants.
    c. with large economies of scale.
    d. with all of the above.

11. Monopolies have the power to
    a. assure investors an economic profit.
    b. block entry.
    c. earn only normal profits.
    d. set the wages of employees.

12. Product differentiation is found in
    a. perfect competition.
    b. monopolistic competition.
    c. oligopoly.
    d. monopoly.

13. Barriers to entry are found in
    a. perfect competition.
    b. monopolistic competition.
    c. oligopoly.
    d. monopoly.

14. Strategic behavior is found in
    a. perfect competition.
    b. monopolistic competition.
    c. oligopoly.
    d. monopoly.

15. Price takers are found in
    a. perfect competition.
    b. monopolistic competition.
    c. oligopoly.
    d. monopoly.

16. Price takers face demand curves that are
    a. perfectly elastic.
    b. perfectly inelastic.
    c. of unit elasticity.
    d. generally downward sloping.

17. Interdependent decision making is found in
    a. perfect competition.
    b. monopolistic competition.
    c. oligopoly.
    d. monopoly.

18. The kinked demand curve is based on the idea that
    a. a firm will follow a cost cut by raising prices.
    b. a firm will follow a price cut but not a price increase.
    c. a firm will follow a price increase but not a price decrease.
    d. a firm makes pricing decisions independent of the pricing of other firms.

19. To sustain a competitive advantage
    a. a market needs entry.
    b. a firm needs to be like its competitors.
    c. a firm needs to earn a normal profit.
    d. needs a barrier to entry.

20. A present value is a measure in
    a. future dollars.
    b. current dollars.
    c. real dollars.
    d. inflated dollars.

Short-Answer Questions

1. What does profit maximization mean?

2. What is marginal revenue?

3. Do monopolies need to consider profit maximization in determining how much to produce?

4. Why might it be profitable for an airline to sell the last seat on a flight to Atlanta for $1?

5. What are some features of a competitive market?

6. What does it mean if my business faces a perfectly elastic demand curve?

7. What is so special about a monopoly?

8. How do the products that are sold on a competitive market compare to the products sold in monopolistic competition?

9. Why is entry so important?

10. What affects the decision to enter a market?

11. Why is strategic behavior found in oligopolies?

12. What is the fundamental premise of the kinked demand curve?

13. Why is a barrier necessary to sustain a competitive advantage?

14. Assume interest rates rise. What happens to present value?

15. What happens to economic profits over the long run in a competitive market?

16. What happens to economic profits over the long run in a monopoly?

Applications and Problems

1. According to the rule of profit maximization, output snould be increased if marginal revenue is greater than marginal cost. Why, if marginal revenue and marginal costs are not equal, do they become equal? Assume that your business sells in a competitive market.

2. What happens to total profits and total losses as firms make output decisions based on marginal revenue and marginal costs.

3. Assume if you bribe a government official, she will grant you a license that will guarantee economic profits for twenty years. What is the most you will pay in bribe?

4. Why is the future worth less when interest rates rise?

5. Could you argue that monopolies don't earn economic profits over the long run?

6. A student came into my office and said that she planned to take my course and not buy the book. I told her that her grade might suffer. Make an economic argument that makes not buying the book sensible.

7. Explain present value to a 10-year-old child. Why is discounting needed?

8. Explain the elasticity of demand inherent in the strategic behavior of the kinked demand curve.

Extending the Case Study: KMART

Joseph Schumpeter, a famous economist whose contributions spanned the 19th and 20th centuries, described the market process as one of "creative destruction." This case is a good example of what Schumpeter had in mind. The recent news concerning KMART has not been good. However, you do not need to look back too far to find good news. KMART was once the new kid on the block with innovation, low prices, differentiation, and marketing imagination with its in-store "blue light specials." McDonald's once had a very simple menu of burgers and fries, did not serve breakfast, had no drive-through service, and offered little in-store seating. It grew rapidly and its success was admired, and then copied, by many. While it remains profitable, McDonald's has changed a lot. The menu has enlarged significantly beyond the traditional fare to include breakfast, healthy salads, etc.; drive-through service is expected, and expanded indoor seating with a play area for children is common.

a.   Why does news change?

b.   Does economic profit lead to changing news?

c.   What insight is provided by Schumpeter's "creative destruction?"

ANSWERS TO ACTIVE REVIEW QUESTIONS

Completion Questions

1.   value
2.   zero
3.   Marginal revenue
4.   expand
5.   MR=MC rule
6.   marginal cost, marginal revenue
7.   framework
8.   market structure
9.   perfect competition, monopolistic competition, oligopoly, monopoly
10.   price taker
11.   price taker, market price
12.   barrier to entry
13.   perfectly elastic
14.   monopoly
15.   block entry
16.   economies of scale
17.   product differentiation
18.   economic profit
19.   oligopoly, strategic behavior
20.   strategic behavior
21.   kinked demand curve, prisoner's dilemma
22.   barrier to entry
23.   present value
24.   discounting
25.   lower

True-False Questions

1.   True   2.   False   3.   True
4.   False   5.   False   6.   True

7. True   8. False   9. False
10. True   11. False   12. True
13. False   14. True   15. True
16. True   17. True   18. False
19. True   20. False   21. True
22. True   23. True   24. False
25. False   26. True   27. True

Multiple-Choice Questions

1. c   2. b   3. a
4. c   5. d   6. b
7. a   8. c   9. a
10. d   11. b   12. b
13. d   14. c   15. a
16. a   17. c   18. b
19. d   20. b

Short-Answer Questions

1. Profit maximization is a decision rule used by economists. It states that output should be expanded if the marginal revenue from selling an additional unit of output is greater than the marginal costs of that output.
2. Marginal revenue is the revenue generated by producing and then selling the next unit of output.
3. Yes. Monopolists must also add value. Just because a firm is a monopoly does not mean that the resources that it uses do not have opportunity costs. The MR=MC rule guides decision making in all markets.
4. In deciding how much to produce, managers need to consider the marginal revenue and the marginal cost of output. It is probably the case that the marginal cost of the next passenger is close to, if not equal to, zero. Therefore, if it is zero, then the $1 goes to profit.
5. Firms in a competitive market are price takers. Their output decisions do not affect the market price. Firms in a competitive market sell homogenous products as well. There is freedom of entry and exit.
6. It means that I am a price taker. I can only sell at the market price. My output decisions will not affect the market price. I will sell nothing if I charge more than the market price.

7. A monopoly can block the entry of others. It means that monopolies are not subject to the same market forces as are firms in a competitive market.

8. Products sold in a competitive market are identical. Products sold in a monopolistically competitive market are not. There is product differentiation.

9. Entry of new firms is how markets change. New firms are attracted to markets where existing firms earn economic profit. With entry, value added is increased for the economy.

10. The presence of economic profits attracts others into a market.

11. Strategic behavior occurs when decision making is interdependent. If, in making a decision, managers consider the response of a rival, then decisions are independent and strategic behavior results.

12. The fundamental premise is that pricing decisions of businesses are not independent of the pricing decisions of rivals. The specific type of strategic behavior is that you, my competitor, will follow my price cut to protect your market share but you will not follow my price increase in order to get my part of my market share.

13. The entry of others takes away economic profit or any advantage a firm might have. Entry causes change.

14. Based on the formula, present value falls. The denominator gets larger, so the sum will get smaller.

15. In a competitive market, economic profits attract other firms. There is entry. With entry, demand for an individual falls as does price. Therefore, entry causes economic profits to disappear.

16. One of the characteristics of a monopoly is that there are barriers to entry. With such barriers, entry can be prevented. Therefore, economic profits can persist over the long run. Entry barriers have value.

Applications and Problems

1. If I am selling in a competitive market, then I am a price taker. Therefore, marginal revenue is equal to the market price. Also, my production decisions will not affect this price – it is constant to me. Marginal costs, on the other hand, do change with production decisions because of the law of diminishing marginal returns. So, if MR is greater than MC, I should expand output. The result is that marginal cost will rise and the difference between it and marginal revenue will diminish. The reverse will happen if marginal revenue is less than marginal costs.

2. If marginal revenue is greater than marginal costs, output should expand. Another way of say this is output should expand if the next unit adds more to total revenue than it adds to total costs. If profits were being earned initially, they will grow further with additional production. If losses were being earned initially, they will get smaller with additional production. So, if MR>MC, then total profits will grow or total losses will get smaller with additional production. If MC>MR, then production cuts will increase total profits or decrease total losses. So, at the point of profit maximization, total profits are the greatest or total losses are the smallest.

3. A license creates a monopoly. Monopolies can block entry and, as such, protect their economic profits. The most I would pay is the present value of the expected economic profits earned over the next twenty years.

4. Rising interest rates reduce the present value of the future. Another way of looking at it is to say that the cost of giving up the present have risen. Rising interest rates are telling you that the future is very expensive.

5. A monopoly has a barrier to entry. This barrier allows the monopoly to earn economic profits over the long run. However, just because it has a barrier does not mean that others won't try to find ways around the barrier. The economic profits on the other side of the barrier are tempting. So, it might be that a monopolist would need to incur costs protecting itself. These cost might eat up the economic prof Others would stop trying to find ways around the barriers only when the economic pr s are gone.

6. First, she would have to buy the book. The price of the book is its marginal cost. It has an opportunity cost. If she adds reading e book to the other study methods she might employ, then the change in her grade is the marginal benefit of the book. If the marginal cost of the book exceeds the marginal benefit of the book, then it pays not to buy the book.

7. You might ask the 10 year old which they would rather have, a dollar today or a dollar next week. Certainly they would want the dollar today. You could ask them why, and they would say that they would rather not wait. The dollar next week is not worth a dollar today. Future dollars and present dollars are not the same. Now offer them 75 cents today or a dollar a week from now. All of a sudden they might think about waiting for the week. As you lower what you will give them today, you will hit an amount where they will be willing to wait. You have just identified their present value.

8. In the kinked demand curve model, if a firm lowers its price, others will follow. Therefore, the firm initiating the price cut finds itself no better off. Because other firms followed, the first firm did not get new customers. Quantity demanded did not change very much – demand is inelastic below the kink. On the other hand, if the first firm raises it price and others do not, then their customers will go elsewhere, quantity demanded may fall by a lot – demand is elastic above the kink.

ANSWERS TO CASE STUDY QUESTIONS

Extending the Case Study: KMART

a. News changes because the economy is dynamic. This makes the continuous earning of economic profit difficult, if not impossible, over the long run. Success brings imitators who try to be just a little bit different.

b. The goal of managers is to add value. When value is added or created, the reward is economic profit. However, economic profits are difficult to maintain. While they are a reward, they are also a signal to others that you are doing something that is valued. In their attempts to earn economic profit, competitors are attracted to what you are doing. Yet, they need to be a little different to give consumers a reason to give them a try. Their difference will force you to be different too. Thus, the nature of the market is changing and its description – the news – will change as well.

c. Schumpeter's "creative destruction" offers insight into the role of economic profits as one of the forces making a market economy dynamic. In their search for economic profits, businesses must create value. This reward for creating added value, however, is its own seeds of destruction. It attracts others. And in the process, new value is created as the old is changed or destroyed. KMART may have been a victim of its own success and the changes at McDonald's may simply be its attempts to survive.

CHAPTER 7

Creating Barriers to Entry

CHAPTER OVERVIEW

One of the recurring themes of the text has been that managers need to focus on adding value when making business decisions. This is seen in the earning of economic profit. While this is all well and good, the presence of economic profits does something else, however. It existence attracts others into the market place. This entry has the effect of making the continual earning of economic profits difficult. In a sense, economic profits sew the seeds to their own destruction. Therefore, firms that are currently earning economic profits find it in their own interests to create barriers to entry or to do things that make it difficult for consumers to consider competitors' products as substitutes. This is to say, they try to block entry. Things such as economies of scale, product differentiation, capital requirements, reputation and brand name are considered as being potential barriers.

KEY CONCEPTS FOR REVIEW

sunk costs   experience goods

search goods   service

rent-seeking   strategic assets

capital requirements   reputation and brand name

ACTIVE REVIEW

Completion Questions

1. _____ cannot be sustained over time unless barriers to entry are created.

2. _____ occur when all resources are increased and per-unit costs fall.

3. If the long run average cost curve is U-shaped, then _____ are followed by _____.

4. For a firm to supply the entire market, it must realize _____ at _____ levels of output.

5. A _____ is an expenditure that has no liquidation value.

6. Advertising expenditures are an example of a _____.

7. When sunk costs are quite large, customers can better trust in a promise of _____.

8. Product differentiation tends to _____ the _____.

9. With differentiation, firms are better able to convert price _____ into increases in _____ given that demand has become more price _____.

10. _____ and _____ are forms of product differentiation.

11. Product or company reputation is a way to communicate information to customers in a _____ way.

12. Finding out information about a product or a company is _____ for consumers.

13. Goods that you learn about as you consume them are called _____.

14. A key component of an experience good is _____.

15. Reliability and experience are two ways that a firm can try to decrease its _____.

16. Goods for which information is obtained with investigation are called _____.

17. A maximum price a consumer is willing to pay may be considered that consumer's _____.

18. A _____ is a good that is consumed as it is produced.

19. Reputation and brand name are valuable when information about _____ is costly.

20. Brand name products are often able to get a _____.

21. The creation of a _____ is a costly activity by a business.

22. _____ and _____ are often used as barriers to entry.

23. Business restrictions developed by _____ can serve as barriers to entry.

24. _____ activities are actions of individuals who attempt to create a barrier to entry by influencing government.

25. De Beers has a barrier to entry because diamonds are a _____.

26. Anything that gives a firm an advantage which is not easily imitable serves as a _____.

True-False Questions

1. T F   Economies of scale can serve as a barrier to entry.

2. T F   If the long run average cost curve is U-shaped, diseconomies of scale are followed by economies of scale.

3. T F   If per-unit cost falls as more of all resources are added to production, then there are diseconomies of scale.

4. T F   If a firm can supply the entire market and be at the lowest point on its long run average cost curve, then there is little room for other smaller firms with higher average costs.

5. T F   Sunk costs have liquidation value.

6. T F   Firms with high sunk costs communicate to potential competitors that they must incur large sunk costs as well if they are to compete effectively.

7. T F   Firms with high sunk costs are not likely to pack up and leave a market.

8. T F   Differentiation is a way to increase the price elasticity of demand.

9. T F   "Intel Inside" is a way to communicate reputation.

10. T F   Brand names are often better able to increase price and thereby increase revenue.

11. T F   A strong brand name good in all likelihood may have a low price elasticity.

12. T F   Search time is free.

13. T F   Search time has opportunity costs.

14. T F   Brand name and reputation can reduce the search time of consumers.

15. T F   Experience goods require consumption to provide information.

16. T F   Reliability and experience goods are not related.

17. T F   Search goods are purchased regularly by consumers.

18. T F   It is reasonable to expect that when consumers purchase a search good, they may have read a publication like *Consumer Reports*.

19. T F   A reservation quality is a minimum.

20. T F   Services can be produced and then consumed at a later date.

21. T F   A lawyer might have a nice office to communicate quality.

22. T F   Brand names are signals that consumers may associate with quality and reputation.

23. T F   Brand names have value.

24. T F   Guarantees are just a cost of doing business and do not serve as a barrier to entry.

25. T F   Government can do little to limit competition.

26. T F   If diamonds had substitutes, then De Beers would not have a unique resource.

27. T F   A dynamic and effective manager would be a strategic asset.

Multiple-Choice Questions

1. A firm is in an advantageous position if it can produce
    a. where economies of scale are increasing.
    b. where long run average cost is at a minimum.
    c. diseconomies of scale are overcome by technology.
    d. only a portion of what the market demands at the current price.

2. Why can economies of scale be a barrier to entry?
    a. Because all the most current technology is being used.
    b. Because diseconomies of scale will never enter into management's decision making.
    c. It is possible to be an effective competitor among many.
    d. It might be possible to supply the entire market at a very low per-unit cost.

3. Large sunk costs
    a. can signal product quality.
    b. make little economic sense as they have no liquidation value.
    c. are the same thing as variable costs.
    d. do little to affect entry and exit.

4. One of the largest sources of sunk costs are
    a. labor costs.
    b. costs of capital.
    c. advertising expenditures.
    d. interest expense on debt instruments.

5. If a firm has successfully differentiated its product, then
    a. price increase will lead to revenue decreases.
    b. price cuts will lead to revenue increases.
    c. price cuts will cause an increase in the quantity demanded.
    d. price increases will lead to revenue increases.

6. Effective reputation and brand recognition could lead to price elasticity of demand
    a. being greater than one.
    b. being less than one.
    c. being equal to one.
    d. becoming inverted.

7. Often, when consumers demand information about a product
    a. successful firms will try to supply more of the product.
    b. successful firms will try to supply it at a low price.
    c. sunk costs should be minimized.
    d. a firm should give as much information as possible to consumers.

8. Incomplete consumer information
    a. is a reason why a firm might try to develop a brand name.
    b. can be completely met by public interest magazines.
    c. is rarely a problem in the area of search goods.
    d. can only be met in a few ways.

9. Goods which require consumption in order to learn about them are
   a. services.
   b. durable goods.
   c. experience goods.
   d. search goods.

10. For which of the following goods might a shopper purchase *Consumer Reports*?
    a. car.
    b. raisins.
    c. higher education.
    d. printer paper.
    e. a and b are possibilities.

11. Price elasticity can be lowered by
    a. lowering price.
    b. raising revenue.
    c. selling a homogenous product.
    d. developing a brand name.

12. Goods that are consumed when they are produced are
    a. experience goods.
    b. services.
    c. search goods.
    d. durables

13. Thomas Watson, founder of IBM, had a dress code for employees in order to
    a. standardize his experience good.
    b. communicate the quality.
    c. minimize variable costs.
    d. copy Xerox.

14. Marketing is often aimed at
    a. lowering price elasticity.
    b. raising price elasticity.
    c. connecting price cuts to revenue increases.
    d. copying competitors.

15. Generic products need to have lower prices because
    a. their price elasticity is unitary.
    b. their price elasticity is low.
    c. their price elasticity is high.
    d. they have a kinked demand curve.

16. A repeat purchase often signals
    a. reputation.
    b. luck.
    c. a high price elasticity.
    d. the demand for a search good.

17. If a firm establishes a guarantee for its product simply because its primary competitor established one, then
    a. there is perfect competition.
    b. the market might be an oligopoly.
    c. there is monopolistic competition.
    d. branding is going on.

18. Why is there rent-seeking by businesses?
    a. Because rental income is usually constant due to leases.
    b. Because firms want open competition.
    c. Because governments can create barriers.
    d. Because consumers want low prices.

19. Tariffs
    a. raise product quality.
    b. level the playing field.
    c. are anti big business.
    d. are a barrier supplied by government.

20. Strategic assets are
    a. never sold.
    b. must be offset by strategic liabilities.
    c. barriers to entry.
    d. are limited to the *Fortune 500*.

Short-Answer Questions

1. Why is it difficult to maintain economic profits?

2. What does it mean when P>ATC?

3. What is the relationship between P and ATC when there are no economic profits?

4. What does it mean to fully exploit your economies of scale?

5. Why would large economies of scale serve as a barrier to entry?

6. Why might advertising assure a consumer that a product is good?

7. What is the point of product differentiation?

8. Why would a firm want to lower its price elasticity through product differentiation?

9. What are some forms of product differentiation?

10. Do consumers try to get perfect information about a product?

11. What is the difference between experience goods, search goods, and services.

12. Does the development of a brand name reduce consumer search time?

13. Why are De Beer's diamonds a unique resource?

Applications and Problems

1. Can there be too much product differentiation?

2. A new restaurant in town wants you to walk around before sitting down and ask diners if they like the food. Why? Would you walk around and talk to other diners?

3. Many times business leaders talk about the wonders and benefits of competition. Are they being sincere?

4. When would business managers be sincere in wanting competition?

5. Make the case that even barriers to entry do not guarantee economic profits over the long run.

6. Why do firms in competitive markets always fully exploit their economies of scale? What are the social consequences of such behavior.

7. Plumbers often list in their telephone book ads that they are bonded. What does this mean and why would they do it?

8. It has been argued throughout the chapter that product differentiation lowers the price elasticity of demand. Why is this the case?

Extending the Case Study: Wal-Mart

Imitation is the highest form of compliment. Economic profits attract imitators. The Wal-Mart case shows that economic returns are generated by managing both parts of the income statement – revenues and costs. Initially, Wal-Mart's success was due to location. Stores were located in communities that no other major retailer served to any significant degree. Today, moving beyond location, the Wal-Mart name is associated with low prices and mega selection. Yet, innovation and the addition of value by Wal-Mart can also be seen in inventory management, information technology, employee training and the like. This is to say, brand name is not necessarily associated with a product. It can also be connected to a process and as well as a concept.

a. How did Wal-Mart deal with the profit-diluting effects of entry?

b. Is profit margin a barrier to entry? Might the name of George Pickett be appropriate to your answer?

c. If you were a small retailer and Wal-Mart came to town, how would you survive? Where would you find an area to add value? Does George Pickett fit in here as well?

d. Are there social consequences to Wal-Mart's behavior and to entry?

ANSWERS TO ACTIVE REVIEW QUESTIONS

Completion Questions

1. Economic profit
2. Economies of scale
3. economies of scale, diseconomies of scale
4. economies of scale, large
5. sunk cost
6. sunk cost
7. high quality
8. reduce, price elasticity of demand
9. increases, revenue, inelastic
10. Reputation, brand name
11. less costly
12. costly
13. experience goods
14. reliability
15. price elasticity of demand
16. search goods
17. reservation price
18. service
19. product quality
20. high price
21. brand name
22. Guarantees, warranties
23. government
24. Rent-seeking
25. unique resource
26. strategic asset

True-False Questions

1.	True	2.	False	3.	False
4.	True	5.	False	6.	True
7.	True	8.	False	9.	True
10.	True	11.	True	12.	False
13.	True	14.	True	15.	True
16.	False	17.	False	18.	True
19.	True	20.	False	21.	True
22.	True	23.	True	24.	False
25.	False	26.	True	27.	True

Multiple-Choice Questions

1.	b	2.	d	3.	a
4.	c	5.	d	6.	b
7.	b	8.	a	9.	c
10.	a	11.	d	12.	b
13.	b	14.	a	15.	c
16.	a	17.	b	18.	c
19.	d	20.	c		

Short-Answer Questions

1. The existence of economic profits attracts others. The entry of others will tend to lower prices and may or may not cause costs to change. The result is that economic profits go away.
2. When price is greater than average total cost, economic profits are being earned.
3. Price and average total costs are equal when economic profits are zero.
4. This means that you should aim to minimize your per-unit costs. Graphically, this would mean that you would want to produce the level of output that minimizes long run average costs.
5. It might be possible for a firm to produce an amount of output that could supply the entire market. New firms would be small and have higher per-unit costs. Therefore, the larger firm would have a competitive advantage over the others which would remain until the others could become as big – if this were even possible.
6. Advertising is a sunk cost. The mere fact that a firm advertises indicates that a sunk cost has been incurred and that it is unlikely that the firm would walk away from the market place.
7. The point of product differentiation is to convince consumers that one product is different from another. Alternatively, that other products are not substitutes. If differentiation is successful, price elasticity of demand is lower.
8. If price elasticity is lowered, demand is becoming more inelastic. As such, firms are then able to raise revenue by raising prices.
9. Forms of product differentiation might include the development of a brand name, reputation, guarantees, warranties, better service, and a different look and feel.
10. No. Information is, in most cases, probably incomplete. Searching for information provides benefits in the form of additional knowledge. Yet searching for information uses resources and, as such, has costs. It is reasonable to suppose that the marginal benefit falls with more searching while marginal search costs rise. Therefore, all searches will not be totally complete and information will not be perfect.
11. Each of these types of goods can be differentiated by the information they provide. Experience goods need to be consumed before consumers can really learning anything about them. While this is also true about services, services can only be consumed when they are produced. Experience goods can be stored before being consumed. Search goods are products that are usually not purchased on a regular basis. An example would be a durable

good like a washing machine. For these goods, consumers spend time learning about them before consuming.

12. Brand names communicate lots of information to consumers. If a particular brand name is associated with quality products and reasonable prices, then consumers would need to spend less time searching for these attributes.

13. There are no substitutes for diamonds. Only when men can show their love for someone with a good quality vacuum cleaner, will the price elasticity of diamonds begin to rise.

Applications and Problems

1. Yes. Differentiation brings benefits to a firm, but it is not free. It uses business resources that have alternative uses. Differentiation should be continued until the benefits from it have been maximized. This would be when the marginal cost from additional differentiation equals the marginal benefits.

2. This would be a way to develop a reputation. However, few people would walk around and talk to others out of a fear of being a pest. The fact that the restaurant encourages you to do it, knowing that you probably won't, is a way to communicate to you that its food is going to be good.

3. Yes, but probably no. Competition means free entry and exit. Therefore, it means that earning economic profits will be very difficult if not impossible. So, if a firm has a very profitable position, it will probably not really want a competitive market.

4. Managers would probably be sincere when they want into a market!

5. Just because a firm has a barrier does not mean that others will not try to find ways around it. Therefore, firms with barriers will need to protect and enforce them. These activities have costs and would eat away at the profits that they are earning. So, the economic profit would not last even with a barrier.

6. When economies of scale are fully exploited, a firm is able to produce at the lowest per-unit cost possible. They, therefore, have a competitive advantage over others – at least for a while. For the economy this means that we are giving up, on average, the least amount of other things to get a particular product. We are getting the most by giving up the least.

7. To be bonded means that your work has a warranty. If there is something wrong with a plumber's work, someone other than the customer will pay to make it right. This is a way to communicate reputation, quality, and to try to minimize the search a customer might make.

8. Product differentiation is a way a firm tries to tell a customer that there are no substitutes for its product. If this is successful, when the firm raises it price, patrons will not go out and look for something else that might provide the same utility.

ANSWERS TO CASE STUDY QUESTIONS

Extending the Case Study: Wal-Mart

a. Wal-Mart did not try to create explicit barriers to entry. Wal-Mart dealt with the profit suppressing effects of entry through innovation. They also have tried to have everything for everyone. So, once a person is in Wal-Mart, there is no need to go anywhere else. This is not unlike gambling casinos giving away food and drinks to patrons. Why go anywhere else if all your needs are being met?

b. Through volume, size, and cost control innovations, Wal-Mart can sell with a low profit margin. If a company wishes to compete head-on with Wal-Mart, it must face the fact that it needs to be as price competitive (unless some other valued point of differentiation is added) and needs to be as innovative on the cost side. Both are sizeable hurdles to leap. So, yes, it is possible that profit margin serves as an implicit barrier to entry. General George Pickett led the Confederate charge up Cemetery Hill on the third day of the Civil War battle at Gettysburg. Pickett's charge failed miserably. The business lesson of his charge is that it makes little sense to make a direct assault on a well-fortified position. Competing head on with Wal-Mart, unless one is able to garner all the needed resources, makes little sense given the size of the overall profit margin of Wal-Mart.

c. There are consultants that help small businesses survive when Wal-Mart comes to town. First, the retailers that survive do not try to meet Wal-Mart head on. They survive by staying on the edges of Wal-Mart's market. One of these is in the area of personal service. Some consumers are willing pay a little bit more for better personalized service which they feel the large Wal-Mart stores do not offer. Wal-Mart is so big that some customers feel lost. Many small local banks compete with much larger national banks by offering such service. Yes, this is an example of learning from Pickett's charge.

d. The social consequences are that value has been added. Wal-Mart keeps its costs low and innovates on the cost side out of self-interest. Yet, the entire economy benefits because Wal-Mart is also minimizing the amount of resources that it uses in the production of its retail empire. Prices are also held low which translates into higher real income for its customers. Others emulate Wal-Mart's behavior to capture an economic return, but society gains also by this behavior.

CHAPTER 8

Price Strategies

CHAPTER OVERVIEW

Managers must make a myriad of decisions and address a multitude of issues. One which seems to get little attention is the development of an effective pricing strategy. In designing a strategy, a decision maker must keep in mind that her goal should be to add value. Managers must find the level of production that maximizes profit. In a one product business, this is found where marginal revenue equals marginal costs. Given this level of output, the appropriate price is the one that clears the profit-maximizing output from the market. The MR=MC rule is fundamental to all effective pricing strategies. This true whether or not the firm is in a competitive commodity market, if it can price discriminate, or if it bundles products. Pricing strategies may become more complex when there are multi-products or when the firms in the market are interdependent. But the point remains, pricing strategy is one of the many things that managers must structure so as to enhance the attainment of the overall goal to add value.

KEY CONCEPTS FOR REVIEW

customizing	personalized pricing
price discrimination	third degree price discrimination
product line extensions	peak load pricing
cost-plus pricing	full cost pricing
pure bundling	mixed bundling
tying	cannibalization
most favored customer, MFC	meet the competition clause, MCC
pricing strategies	bid/ask auction
reverse auction	value pricing
framing	limit price
predatory pricing	transfer prices
price war	odd pricing

ACTIVE REVIEW

Completion Questions

1. _____ are as important as decisions concerning cost containment.

2. Exchanges over the internet are also called _____.

3. An auction where a seller sets an asking price and buyers try to outbid each other is called a _____.

4. A seller auction is also known as a _____.

5. Price determination in an auction is very similar to price determination in a _____.

6. Auctions and increase information enhance the value of _____.

7. When there is differentiation, price is greater than _____.

8. The quantity that maximizes profit is found by equating _____ and _____.

9. High and low prices often affect consumer perceptions about _____.

10. The concept of _____ reflects the role of differentiation in pricing.

11. When pricing strategy focuses on unique customers, time of the day, etc., pricing is said to be _____.

12. When each customer can be charged a different price for the same product, the business is practicing _____.

13 If groups can be separated by different price elasticities of demand, a firm is able to practice _____.

14. The profit maximizing quantity and the demand curve will determine the _____ a firm will try to charge.

15. Often, _____ are used to have consumers separate themselves into separate market segments and pay different prices for the same product.

16. Electric utilities use _____ to raise rates during the hottest time of the day.

17. When a firm adds a markup to the costs of producing a product, it is practicing _____ or _____.

18. Cost-plus pricing does not often lead to _____.

19. Markups tend to rise as price elasticity tends to _____.

20. Firms will _____ their price in order to exploit consumer perceptions and to set a context for price changes.

21. If the price of a pizza is $5.98, rather than $6.00, the producer is using

   _____.

22. _____ is used to drive competitors out of a market.

23. When a firm tries to sell a combination of products compared to selling each product separately, it is _____ their output.

24. In pure bundling, a producer is not able to _____ among customers.

25. Profits can be enhanced if _____ is used as opposed to pure bundling.

26. If you must buy paper from a company in order to buy its printer, the producer is

   _____.

27. _____ occurs when sales of one product produced by a firm reduce the demand for another product produced by the same firm.

28. When one division of a company sells to another division within the same company, a _____ is charged.

29. Profit centers are parts of a company which must individually _____.

30. In an oligopoly, _____ will affect pricing strategy.

31. "We will not be undersold" is an example of _____.

True-False Questions

1. T   F   A pricing strategy is an integral part of adding value

2. T   F   Price determination in an internet auction is similar to price determination in an oligopoly.

3. T   F   In a bid/ask scheme a buyer sets a price and sellers compete for their business.

4. T   F   A reverse auction is also a seller's auction

5. T   F   In an internet auction, price and marginal revenue are usually equal.

6. T   F   In some industries, technology is used in price determination and has replaced the "gut feel" approach to pricing.

7. T   F   A restaurant that charges higher prices during its busiest hours is practicing personalized pricing.

8. T   F   One finds price discrimination in a competitive market.

9. T   F   The value of differentiation is unaffected by the pricing strategy managers use.

10. T   F   Ineffective pricing strategies "leave money on the table."

11. T F   Producers can use product line extensions to have customers separate themselves into different groups.

12. T F   Peak-load pricing is synonymous with cost-plus pricing.

13. T F   Markups are positively related to price elasticity.

14. T F   Full cost pricing maximizes profits.

15. T F   In cost-plus pricing, a price is a markup of average cost.

16. T F   Producers are indifferent between announcing price increases and announcing price decreases.

17. T F   Odd pricing has been used to control employee theft.

18. T F   Pricing can be used as a barrier to entry.

19. T F   Predatory pricing is when a small firm undercuts a large firm in order to get a toe hold in a market.

20. T F   Bundling products often enhances revenue over the revenue earned by selling products separately.

21. T F   The effectiveness of bundling is enhanced if every consumer has the average demand curve.

22. T F   Pure bundling uses discrimination.

23. T F   Mobile phone companies tie the purchase of a phone to the activation fee.

24. T F   Profits are enhanced if transfer prices can be raised above external market prices.

25. T F   Price wars are found when pricing decisions between competitors are interdependent.

26. T F   "Meet the competition" clauses are attempts to keep customers from shopping around among competitors for the best price.

Multiple-Choice Questions

1. Which of the following is not an important business decision?
    a. Cost containment.
    b. Introducing new products.
    c. Pricing strategies.
    d. Possible mergers.
    e. All of the above are important.

2. The pricing dynamics in a internet auction tend to resemble which market?
    a. Oligopoly.
    b. Monopolistic competition.
    c. Perfect competition.
    d. Monopoly and perfect competition

3. Pricing strategies most directly affect
    a. variable costs.
    b. sales revenue.
    c. marginal costs.
    d. economies of scale.

4. In a bid/ask auction scheme
    a. buyers set prices and sellers attempt to match them.
    b. sellers and buyers file sealed bids.
    c. buyers ask and sellers bid.
    d. sellers set an asking price and buyers try to outbid each other.

5. Priceline.com best resembles a
    a. name-your-own-price auction.
    b. bid/ask auction.
    c. reverse auction.
    d. straight consumer auction.

6. In a competitive market
    a. price is less than marginal revenue.
    b. price is equal to marginal revenue.
    c. price is greater than marginal revenue.
    d. price and marginal revenue are not related.

7. When there is product differentiation
    a. price is less than marginal cost.
    b. price is equal to marginal cost.
    c. price is greater than marginal costs.
    d. price and marginal revenue are not related.

8. Profits are maximized when
    a. marginal revenue and marginal cost are equal.
    b. marginal revenue is greater than marginal cost.
    c. marginal cost is greater than marginal revenue.
    d. marginal revenue equals price.

9. Pricing strategies must recognize the possibility
    a. of multi-product offerings.
    b. interdependence between competitors.
    c. too high a price might attract new entrants.
    d. of all of the above happening.

10. When a firm personalizes its price, it is able to
    a. control variable costs.
    b. enhance revenue.
    c. raise elasticity.
    d. use auctions to identify customers.

11. If a firm is able to charge different buyers different prices for the same product, it is able to
    a. use auctions for bidding.
    b. enter a competitive market.
    c. price discriminate.
    d. have uniform pricing.

12. If firms are able to group customers with similar elasticities and then charge each group a different price, the firm is able to
    a. price discriminate.
    b. enter a competitive market.
    c. have uniform pricing.
    d. use auctions for bidding.

13. Price discrimination is only effective if
    a. the firm can control costs.
    b. the separate groups cannot communicate with each other.
    c. the government is unaware of it.
    d. products are homogenous.

14. Product line extensions are similar to
    a. cost containment.
    b. minimizing long run average fixed costs.
    c. price discrimination.
    d. using elasticity to measure the effectiveness of a marketing campaign.

15. Firms that experience fluctuations in demand over time may be able to
    a. extend their product line.
    b. cost-plus price.
    c. mark-up price.
    d. peak-load price.

16. When a firm uses a cost-plus pricing strategy, price is determined by the following expression:
    a. P = (marginal cost)(1+markup).
    b. P = (marginal cost)(markup).
    c. P = (average costs)(1+markup).
    d. P = (average cost/marginal cost)(1=markup).

17. The amount of a markup and price elasticity of demand
    a. are inversely related.
    b. are directly related.
    c. are not related.
    d. are proportionally related.

18. At times, price can be used to
    a. signal quality.
    b. prevent entry.
    c. encourage entry.
    d. all of the above are possible.

19. When pricing is used to drive competitors out of the market, the strategy is one of
    a. cost markup.
    b. predatory pricing.
    c. aggressive pricing.
    d. meeting the competition.

20. Mixed and pure bundling is used to
    a. raise elasticity.
    b. enhance revenue.
    c. reduce cannibalization.
    d. promote sales of individual units

21. When a drive-through restaurant asks you if you would like to try their special combination lunch, they are practicing
    a. cost-plus pricing.
    b. peak-load pricing.
    c. pure bundling.
    d. mixed bundling.

22. Transfer prices are
    a. prices that divisions of the same company charge each other.
    b. only found on tied goods.
    c. found in markets external to the business.
    d. fees of moving companies.

23. When units of the same company are managed so that "every tub has its own bottom"
    a. then each is producing a joint product.
    b. then each unit can cannibalize the others.
    c. then multiple products will get produced efficiently.
    d. then each is a profit center.

24. Interdependence among firms is found in
    a. perfect competition.
    b. mixed bundling.
    c. oligopoly.
    d. monopolistic competition.

25. "We will not be undersold" is an example of
    a. price fixing.
    b. a "meet the competition" clause.
    c. a most-favored customer clause.
    d. cost-plus pricing.

Short-Answer Questions

1. Why do pricing strategies matter?

2. On a fundamental level, how does a producer determine what price to charge?

3. Describe a bid/ask auction scheme.

4. What does it mean for a market to become commoditized?

5. How is price determined in a competitive market?

6. How does a single seller in a competitive market view price and marginal revenue?

7. How does a single seller view price and marginal revenue when there is product differentiation in the market?

8. Describe perfect price discrimination.

9. Why would a firm want to price discriminate?

10. Why do publishers offer hardback books first and then lower priced paperback versions?

11. Why might Coke even think of developing machines that varied the price based on the surrounding temperature?

12. It is probably the case that cost-plus pricing is the most widely observed pricing strategy. Why?

13. Why is the markup used in cost-plus pricing related to price elasticity of demand?

14. Can a pricing strategy be a barrier to entry?

15. Why would a producer bundle?

16. In a product line extension it is important to avoid cannibalization. Why?

17. What would be a simple pricing strategy for setting transfer prices between profit centers.

18. Why are price wars possible in oligopolies?

19. Why do "meet the competition" strategies make price less important in competition?

20. What is the difference between pure and mixed bundling?

Applications and Problems

1. Restaurants keep waiting lists on busy nights. At times the wait can be for as long as an hour of two. Design a pricing strategy that is an alternative to the waiting list. How might elasticity fit into your answer?

2. Several years ago as part of a no-smoking campaign, the few cigarette manufacturers agreed to not advertise in certain venues like television and magazines aimed at teens. None of the manufacturers protested. Why?

3. Do changes in fixed costs affect pricing policies over the short run?

4. In the text it states that price and marginal revenue are equal in competitive markets but that price is greater than marginal revenue when there is product differentiation. Why? Assume that you are given the following information, calculate marginal revenue and relate your answer to elasticity

Perfect Competition		Product Differentiation	
Q	P/unit	Q	P/unit
1	$5	1	$110
2	5	2	90
3	5	3	80
4	5	4	70
5	5	5	60

6	5	6	50
7	5	7	40
8	5	8	30

5. Many stores now use scanner technology to check out customers at the time of sale. Each price tag has a computer code that contains the price among other things. if possible, why would stores rather scan the head of consumers instead of the price tag? What does this do to consumer surplus?

6. Assume a college serves both a night and a day market. Assume that the day demand is $P = 3000 - 6Q$, and that marginal revenue is $MR = 3000 - 12Q$. Also assume that the demand for night classes is $P = 1500 - Q$ while marginal revenue is $MR = 1500 - 2Q$. The marginal cost of teaching students is 500. What should be the day and night tuition and how many students will maximize profits? What must the college control for?

Extending the Case Study: Pricing Chips

This case brings together many things that have been discussed in the first few chapter of the text. As has been said many times, and will be said many more, the goal of management should be to maximize economic profit by adding value. From the case, the Phoenix tortilla chip producer initially succeeded in doing just this. It survived in the face of competition from Frito-Lay, a major national corporation.

From the view of an accountant, profitability is measured through the income statement. The income statement has two general parts, revenue and costs. This case is addressing revenue issues. Revenue has two parts. First, is the per-unit price of the product. Over time, both the Phoenix producer and Frito-Lay raised the per-unit price. The second part of revenue is the quantity that is sold at the per-unit price. As the Phoenix producer raised its price, the quantity demanded fell to an extent that the chip maker stopped operations. Thus, the interaction between price and quantity demanded – price elasticity of demand – is an essential issue of this case. This case has returned us to "knowing the customer, " but now we are learning about our buyers through our pricing strategies.

a. In choosing between substitutes, do consumers buy the absolutely cheapest product?

b. With respect to price, how do consumers choose between substitutes.

c. How does a pricing strategy relate to "knowing the customer?"

ANSWERS TO ACTIVE REVIEW QUESTIONS

Completion Questions

1. Pricing strategies
2. on-line auctions
3. bid/ask scheme

4.   reverse auction
5.   competitive market
6.   product differentiation
7.   marginal revenue
8.   marginal revenue, marginal cost
9.   quality
10. value pricing
11. personalized
12. perfect price discrimination
13. second or third degree price discrimination
14. price
15. product line extensions
16. peak-load pricing
17. cost-plus pricing, full cost pricing
18. maximizing profits
19. fall
20. frame
21. odd pricing
22. Predatory pricing
23. bundling
24. discriminate
25. mixed bundling
26. tying
27. Cannibalization
28. transfer price
29. maximize profit
30. interdependence
31. meeting the competition

True-False Questions

1.	True	2.	False	3.	False
4.	True	5.	True	6.	True
7.	True	8.	False	9.	False
10.	True	11.	True	12.	False
13.	False	14.	False	15.	True
16.	False	17.	True	18.	True
19.	False	20.	True	21.	False
22.	False	23.	True	24.	False
25.	True	26.	True		

Multiple-Choice Questions

1.	e	2.	c	3.	b
4.	d	5.	a	6.	b
7.	c	8.	a	9.	d
10.	b	11.	c	12.	a
13.	b	14.	c	15.	d
16.	c	17.	a	18.	d
19.	b	20.	b	21.	d
22.	a	23.	d	24.	c
25.	b				

Short-Answer Questions

1. Pricing strategies matter as they determine the total revenue of a producer. An effective pricing strategy indicates that the producer "knows the customer."

2. The first thing a producer must do is to determine how much to produce – the profit maximizing quantity. This is found by equating marginal revenue and marginal cost. Once this quantity is determined it is related to the demand that the producer faces. The price that is charged is the one that clears the profit maximizing quantity from the market.

3. In a bid/ask auction scheme, the seller sets an asking price and buyers try to outbid each other.

4. It means that the market is becoming more like perfect competition. Each seller is becoming a price-taker.

5. Price will move toward the level which equates the quantity demanded of a good or service to the quantity supplied. When the quantity supplied is greater than the quantity demanded, price will fall. Price will rise when the quantity demanded is greater than the quantity supplied.

6. In a competitive market, price and marginal revenue are equal.

7. Product differentiation makes the single seller a price maker. When this occurs price is greater than marginal revenue.

8. Under perfect price discrimination, a firm is able to identify the highest price each customer is willing and able to pay and then charge it.

9. Price discrimination enhances revenue. Firms try to classify buyers into groups based on their price elasticities of demand. Firms will try to charge groups higher prices if they have low price elasticity.

10. Some readers prefer hardback books and are willing and able to pay more for them compared to readers who really don't care about the form their book takes. This latter group is more price sensitive. As such, publishers get more revenue under this scheme than if it just offered hardbacks or just offered paperbacks. This is a form of product line extension.

11. Coke seems to "know its customer." Temperature is a determinant of demand for soft drinks. On a hot day, a cold Coke is in greater demand than on a cold winter day. Demand is greater and probably more inelastic. Therefore, Coke could probably charge more on a hot day than

on a cold day. Price would vary to reflect this change in demand. This is an example of peak-load pricing.

12. It is very simple.

13. The higher the markup, the higher the price. If price elasticity of demand is low or inelastic it is easier for firms to charge higher prices. Therefore, the lower the elasticity the higher the markup.

14. If an incumbent has lower costs than potential entrants, then it might be possible to keep price low, and others may find it unprofitable to enter the market. At the extreme there is predatory pricing where a large seller keeps price low so as to drive out smaller competitors.

15. Producers bundle to enhance revenue. This is to say, the revenue from bundling two products would generate more revenue compared to that which would be earned if the products were sold separately.

16. Cannibalization occurs when the sale of one product of a producer reduces the demand for another product of the same producer. Therefore, when the product line is extended, the new product should not compete with the first product. It is important that the products in an extension are selling to different market segments.

17. A transfer price can be no more than the price for the same item on an external market. If it is more, the profit center buying the item will become less profitable. This defeats the purpose of having profit centers.

18. Interdependence is the key characteristic of an oligopoly. Given the importance of pricing strategies in general and if firms are interdependent, it make sense that the pricing policies of one firm will affect the policies of the others and vice versa. If one firm starts to cut prices, others will need to follow to protect their respective market shares, and a price war might result.

19. "We guarantee to meet the competition" means that a firm will sell a product at the lowest price in the market if a customer finds one. Therefore, customers know that they will get the lowest price in the market. Knowing this is a guarantee; consumers do not need to spend search time looking for the lowest price. It almost becomes incidental to their search. Other items that are valued like service, hours of operation, etc., become more important.

20. Pure bundling is the idea that only the package of bundled goods can be purchased. Mixed bundling is the practice of offering both the package of bundled goods and the goods in the bundle separately. Mixed bundling is more common when a seller is able to discriminate between customers and their respective elasticity.

Applications and Problems

1. The waiting lists indicate excess demand at existing prices. An alternative to the lists would be to have different prices at different times of the day. The highest prices would be found during the busiest time of the day. This is a peak-load pricing problem. The busiest periods would probably have relatively inelastic demand. Some restaurants have lower prices during the very early evenings. They find that low prices tend to increase revenue during these hours. This suggests an elastic demand curve.

2. The failure to complain is based on the interdependence of the few manufacturers. If one could not advertise in these selected venues, then it was alright as long as it competitors could not do the same.

3. The optimum price is found by equating marginal revenue and marginal cost. Marginal cost is defined as the change in total cost or the change in total variable cost when output is changed. Fixed costs do not change with output and, as such, would not be part of marginal

cost. Changes in fixed costs would not affect price. However, changes in fixed costs would affect the size of profits or losses earned at the profit-maximizing level of production.

4. The chart shows a very important issue. In perfect competition, the price facing an individual seller is constant. They are a price taker. When there is product differentiation, the market moves away from perfect competition and individual firms become price makers. This is to say, to sell more they must lower price. This is the reason why price is greater than marginal cost.

Perfect Competition				Product Differentiation			
Q	P/unit	TR	MR	Q	P/unit	TR	MR
0	$5	0		0	$110	0	
1	5	5	5	1	100	100	100
2	5	10	5	2	90	180	80
3	5	15	5	3	80	240	60
4	5	20	5	4	70	280	40
5	5	25	5	5	60	300	20
6	5	30	5	6	50	300	0
7	5	35	5	7	40	280	-20
8	5	40	5	8	30	240	-40

As you move down the chart for perfect competition, price remains constant. You can see that price and marginal revenue are equal. In the other chart, price falls in order to sell more. At first revenue rises as price falls. Also, marginal revenue is positive. Alternatively, demand is elastic. However, as price continues to fall, revenue starts to fall and marginal revenue is negative. Demand has become price inelastic.

5. Scanning the head of a customer might reveal the most the customer is willing and able to pay for a particular item. The store would like to charge this price and price discriminate. They can't, however. If they charge too much, consumers will go elsewhere. The difference between what a consumer is willing to pay and the market price is called consumer surplus. Consumers gain this when they buy in a competitive market. However, when a firm price discriminates, they are able the convert the consumer surplus into revenue for themselves.

6. First thing to do is set marginal revenue equal to marginal cost and then solve for Q. Then substitute this Q into the demand equation and solve for P.

   Day: $3000 - 12Q = 500$; $Q = 208$; $P = 1752$

   Night: $1500 - Q = 500$; $Q = 1000$; $P = 100$

   The college must try to keep day students from becoming night students. It must be careful to keep the markets separate.

ANSWERS TO CASE STUDY QUESTIONS

Extending the Case Study: Pricing Chips

a. Products are substitutes if the utility consumers get from consuming one good can be replaced by consuming another good. Two goods are perfect substitutes if the only difference between them is price. All other aspects of the two goods are absolutely identical. While some products exhibit this likeness, most products are a little different is some way. In this case, the products are close substitutes. In this situation, consumers do not necessarily buy the product that has the absolutely lowest price. Consumers will trade off a lower price for perceived value. If the Phoenix producer's chips were perfect substitutes for the Frito-Lay brand, then no Frito-Lay tortilla chips would have been sold. This was not the case.

b. Consumers choose between close substitutes based on relative, not absolute, prices. They judge one price in terms of another. They also consider other attributes besides price. Even though both chip producers raised their prices, the relative price of Frito-Lay chips fell. Because of this, chip buyers substituted the Frito-Lay brand for the locally produced brand. Apparently, the additional quality of the local brand was not sufficient to overcome this increase in its relative price. As such, the quality difference no longer added value, and the company failed.

c. Revenue is per-unit price multiplied by the quantity sold. That is, revenue is determined from the demand curve. The demand curve shows the behavior of a company's customers. This behavior is seen in their buying patterns which is determined by our pricing strategy, all other things constant. So, an effective price strategy is made while "knowing the customer."

CHAPTER 9

The New Economy: Technological Change and Innovation

CHAPTER OVERVIEW

Much has been made of the "new economy." Such a system has been brought about by the technological changes and informational interfaces of the past decade. Characteristics include the decomposition of the supply chain, winner-take-all events, tipping points, networks, positive feedback, and positive network externalities. But, as is often the case, new ideas, concepts, and jargon can be traced back to the "old economy" and to fundamental economic principles. It is apparent from the chapter that the old French saying is correct: "The more things change, the more they stay the same.

KEY CONCEPTS FOR REVIEW

new economy	networks
positive feedback	positive network externalities
winner-takes-all	tipping point
locked-in	path dependence
basic research	applied research
development	decomposed
contagiousness	sunk-cost effect

ACTIVE REVIEW

Completion Questions

1. The _____ refers to the technological changes that have occurred in information processing and management.

2. _____ is always with us – it is simply part of the human spirit to want more than there is available.

3. During the 1990s the _____ of many businesses were destroyed or decomposed.

4. The supply change is _____ when the information content of a product can be separated from the physical product itself.

5. A major characteristic of the new economy is the importance of _____.

6. A _____ is an alliance of firms or it can be a standard to which several businesses comply.

7. _____ refers to the idea that the benefits of an individual joining a network go to every member of the network, not just the member joining.

8. Positive feedback is also referred to as _____.

9. Positive feedback tends to _____ demand.

10. The more members in a network, the _____ is the value of membership to an additional member.

11. The sales of some products have shown a pattern similar to an _____.

12. A _____ shows a pattern that the sales of some products have exhibited.

13. In an epidemic, little changes have _____ effects.

14. The _____ is that moment an explosion in numbers occurs and the diffusion process accelerates.

15. There are times when only one competitor can survive. This event is called _____.

16. If demand increases so that _____ persist throughout the market, then one firm or one network will survive.

17. _____ is when an historical accident or random event plays favor with some technology.

18. QWERTY is an example of _____.

19. Some technology, once learned, can become _____.

20. Something is _____ when the costs of not being infected are greater than the costs of being infected.

21. If a manger wants to try to create an epidemic for her product, she should focus on the _____.

22. When two or more incompatible technologies struggle to become a standard, they are engaged in a _____.

23. To win a standards war, you must have a distinct capability that has _____.

24. Two types of research are _____ and _____.

25. When new technology is adopted, _____ is reduced.

26. The essence of the _____ is that one learns how to reduce production costs through actual production experience so that the more a firm produces, the lower its average costs.

27. Dominant firms tend to lag in the introduction of innovations due to the _____.

True-False Questions

1. T F   The absence of scarcity is the main characteristic of the new economy.

2. T F   Technological changes in information helped decompose the supply chains of many producers.

3. T F   Banking is one industry that has avoided the decomposition of the supply chain.

4. T F   Technological change in information will affect products whose information content can be separated from the physical product itself.

5. T F   The presence of networks is a main feature of the new economy.

6. T F   A network is an alliance of firms or a standard to which several businesses comply.

7. T F   Successful networks offer negative network externalities.

8. T F   The benefits of joining a network extend to others already in the network.

9. T F   Given that it is hard to communicate across networks, the benefits of joining a network are inversely related to its size.

10. T F   The presence of positive externalities serves to increase demand.

11. T F   A diffusion process can be used to explain the patterns of epidemics.

12. T F   The saturation point is where sales explode.

13. T F   The diffusion process can be shown by a "V-shaped" curve.

14. T F   The point of explosion in a diffusion process is called the tipping point.

15. T F   If economies of scale continue to expand as the diffusion process continues, it is unlikely that a winner-takes-all event will occur.

16. T F   QWERTY is an example of path dependence.

17. T F   A path dependence reliance on a certain technology cannot be locked-in.

18. T F   Entrepreneurs can generally find ways to deal with lock-in that is not efficient.

19. T F   Things are contagious when the costs of being infected are less than the costs of not being infected.

20. T F   A marginal change is a large accumulation of changes.

21. T F   Marginal analysis is one of the innovations to come out of the new economy.

22. T   F   The winner of a standards war must have a valued difference.

23. T   F   Prices in the new economy are set in the same way they were set in the old economy.

24. T   F   Technological change causes the long run average total cost curve to shift.

25. T   F   Initial innovators have probably incurred the lowest development costs.

26. T   F   Experience curves cause the sunk-cost effect.

27. T   F   Business size may be related to the sunk-cost effect.

Multiple-Choice Questions

1. The new economy is largely based in technological innovations in
   a. management.
   b. economics.
   c. marketing.
   d. government regulations.

2. Scarcity is
   a. an old economy problem only.
   b. something found in only developing countries.
   c. in the old and the new economies.
   d. less of a problem due to informational innovations.

3. When the informational content of a product is separated from the physical product itself,
   a. advertising is needed.
   b. the supply chained has been decomposed.
   c. the demand curve is becoming more inelastic.
   d. scarcity has been reduced.

4. A characteristic of the new economy is seen in the
   a. increased importance of networks.
   b. decrease in the need to supply chain manage.
   c. appearance of scarcity.
   d. absence of informational innovation.

5. It is argued that networks have positive feedback.
   a. This means that email is faster.
   b. This means that complaints are handled faster.
   c. This indicates the presence of a negative externality.
   d. This means there are positive network externalities.

6. A positive externality is
   a. a cost not paid.
   b. a benefit not received.
   c. a benefit received but not paid for.
   d. a benefit-revenue linkage.

7. A positive network externality means that
    a. the benefits of an individual joining the network go to every member of the network, not just the member joining.
    b. the benefits of an individual joining the network are totally internalized.
    c. the benefits of an individual joining the network are averaged out over everyone.
    d. the revenue of the ISP is larger.

8. Positive externalities cause
    a. an increase in supply.
    b. an increase in the quantity demanded.
    c. an decrease in the quantity supplied.
    d. an increase in demand.

9. The pattern of an epidemic can be described as a
    a. "V"- shaped curve.
    b. diffusion process.
    c. injunctive process.
    d. market.

10. In terms of sales, at the tipping point,
    a. sales decrease.
    b. sales increase at an increasing rate.
    c. sales start to rise.
    d. the run is over.

11. When a market has tipped
    a. sales growth as ended.
    b. sales have started.
    c. standardization has occurred.
    d. differentiation is present.

12. When a market tips
    a. one network or firms supply.
    b. the winner-takes-all strategy has failed.
    c. prices become meaningless.
    d. differentiation is present.

13. In a winner-takes-all event
    a. diseconomies of scale occur at low output.
    b. economies of scale are large enough to satisfy the market.
    c. tipping is never considered.
    d. per-unit costs rise.

14. Path dependence
    a. represents good planning.
    b. is independent of the randomness in the world
    c. always reflects efficiency.
    d. can be just an accident.

15. QWERTY
    a. is an example of positive feedback.
    b. is a successful ISP network.
    c. is an example of path dependence.
    d. has been shown to be efficient.

16. Something is contagious when
    a. the costs of not being infected are greater than the costs of being infected.
    b. the costs of not being infected are less than the costs of being infected.
    c. the costs of not being infected are equal to the costs of being infected.
    d. the benefits of infection are low.

17. Standards wars
    a. never end.
    b. are often won by the technology with the most value.
    c. must be settled by the government.
    d. violate patents.

18. Pricing in the new economy
    a. is different compared to the old economy.
    b. is based on less scarcity.
    c. is the same as in the old economy.
    d. is done more in monopolies than in the old economy.

19. Research with an expected practical payoff is
    a. applied research.
    b. basic research.
    c. fundamental research.
    d. general research.

20. Technological change will
    a. cause prices to fall even when demand increases
    b. always cause marginal costs to rise.
    c. lead to an increase in demand.
    d. will possibly lower per-unit costs.

21. Patents
    a. are generally path dependent.
    b. cause lock-in.
    c. are barriers to entry.
    d. are never very profitable given the long approval period.

22. Learning curves
    a. are only found in large firms.
    b. affect per-unit costs.
    c. cause fixed costs to shift in the short run.
    d. are a fundamental part of path dependence.

23. Innovations are generally not introduced by large firms
    a. because they already have the market share they want.
    b. because they are already successful.
    c. because of the variable cost effect.
    d. because of the sunk-costs effect.

Short-Answer Questions

1. What are two characteristics of the new economy?
2. What is the "new economy?"
3. What happens when the supply chain is decomposed?
4. What is a network?
5. What is the positive feedback of a network?
6. What is a positive externality and how does it relate to a network?
7. What is a diffusion process?
8. What are two characteristics of epidemics?
9. What is a tipping point?
10. When can a winner-takes-all event occur?
11. What happens if it is costly to switch networks or if cross-network communication is not possible?
12. What is path dependence and how does it related to being locked-in?
13. When is something contagious?
14. How can a manager contribute to making her product contagious?
15. What is a standards war?
16. What is the difference between applied and basic research?
17. Is a patent race a winner-takes-all event?
18. What is a learning curve?
19. Why might a dominant firm not be the source of new innovation?

Applications and Problems

1. In the text, the diffusion process is shown graphically by an "S-shaped" curve. Describe what this shape means. Have you seen it in an earlier chapter? Use sales as the context for your answer.
2. Will on-line colleges eventually replace traditional colleges?
3. It was argued in the text that a positive externality will increase demand. What will it do to supply?
4. How is price set in the new economy?
5. Patents are exclusive rights to produce something for a given period of time. Let's look at the importance of "for a given period of time" for a moment. The government grants patents

once an application is received and approved. Does it matter if the patent clock starts when the patent is submitted for approval or starts when the patent is approved?

6. Some argue that a QWERTY world is proof that markets don't work noting that inefficient technologies are never replaced. Use a cost-benefit framework to counter this argument.

7. After a friend of mine was awarded a patent, he hired a new patent lawyer to find ways around the patent. Why would he have done this given the fact that he already had a patent?

Extending the Case Study: Winner Takes All

Some claim that winner-takes-all events have characterized the "new economy." The competition between the alternative suppliers of broadband technology – DSL or cable – is the focus of the case. The case concludes by arguing that three conditions for a winner-takes-all event have not been met. There are economies of scale, but they seem to be available to each of the alternatives. In addition, the conditions of positive network externalities and little or no demand for variety are not sufficiently strong to set the environment for winner-takes-all.

a. A winner-takes-all event did occur between VHS and Beta over format for VCR tapes. Would the fact that VHS and Beta required different machines matter?

b. Let us suppose that the battle between DSL and cable met the conditions for a winner-takes-all event. Would the ultimate winner have a monopoly with a barrier to entry? Is competition limited? If not, how would it be seen?

c. Can your answer to b. be related to a.?

ANSWERS TO ACTIVE REVIEW QUESTIONS

Completion Questions

1. new economy
2. Scarcity
3. supply chain
4. decomposed
5. networks
6. network
7. Feedback
8. positive network externalities
9. increase
10. greater
11. epidemic
12. diffusion process
13. big
14. tipping point
15. winner-takes-all
16. economies of scale
17. Path dependence

18. path dependence
19. locked-in
20. contagious
21. margin
22. standards war
23. value
24. basic, applied
25. long run average cost
26. experience curve
27. sunk-cost effect

True-False Questions

1.	False	2.	True	3.	False
4.	True	5.	True	6.	True
7.	False	8.	True	9.	False
10.	True	11.	True	12.	False
13.	False	14.	True	15.	False
16.	True	17.	False	18.	True
19.	True	20.	False	21.	False
22.	True	23.	True	24.	True
25.	False	26.	False	27.	True

Multiple-Choice Questions

1.	c	2.	c	3.	b
4.	a	5.	d	6.	c
7.	a	8.	d	9.	b
10.	b	11.	c	12.	a
13.	b	14.	d	15.	c
16.	a	17.	b	18.	c
19.	a	20.	d	21.	c
22.	b	23.	d		

Short-Answer Questions

1. Two characteristics of the new economy include the decomposition of the supply chain and the appearance of networks.
2. The "new economy" refers to the technological changes that have occurred in information processing and management.
3. When the supply chain is decomposed the information content of the product is separated from the physical product itself.
4. A network is an alliance of firms, or it can be a "standard" to which several businesses comply.
5. The positive feedback of a network is referring to the idea that the benefits of an individual joining a network go to every member of the network, and not just to the member joining.
6. A positive externality is a benefit that is received for which someone did not pay. I pay to access a network. Yet, when someone else joins, the value of the network increases for me.
7. A diffusion process is a pattern that a series of events could follow. For example, initially sales begin slowly, and then, after hitting a tipping point, they explode. This growth finally slows at the saturation point.
8. Epidemics are contagious. Next, little changes have big effects.
9. It is the point at which the growth in some process explodes.
10. A winner-takes-all event can occur if, as demand grows, a producer continues to experience economies to scale until market demand has been filled.
11. This makes the benefits of being in the largest network greater. It is also possible that a winner-takes-all event might occur.
12. Path dependence is when some historical accident or random event plays favor with some technology. This technology then becomes a standard and used even if it is not the most efficient. As a standard, people get locked-in to its use – like the arrangement of keys on a typical keyboard.
13. Something is contagious when the costs of not being infected are greater than the costs of being infected.
14. They should try to reduce the net costs of being infected or raise the costs of not being infected.
15. A standards war exists when two or more incompatible technologies struggle to become the acceptable standards.
16. Basic research is aimed at the creation of new knowledge while applied research is usually aimed at having a practical payoff. Many profit-seeking businesses engage in applied research.
17. Yes. A patent is an exclusive right, at least for a limited number of years. Others can be excluded. Therefore, a patent race in a winner-takes-all event.
18. A learning curve describes the process that as more and more output is produced over time and experience is gained, the cost per unit of output falls.
19. This is due to the sunk cost effect. The dominant firm has already invested lots of resources in a particular technology or organizational capabilities, so that they are less likely to make changes that make this investment worthless.

Applications and Problems

1. The "S-shaped" curve indicates that after launching a new product, sales begin to increase slowly. With time, the rate of growth of sales starts to increase at an increasing rate at the tipping point and beyond. Then the growth of sales slows to the point of saturation where sales have peaked. If you look at the rate of change in the curve, it reflects the law of diminishing marginal returns that was presented in the chapter on costs. This link also allows you to see how important marginal analysis is to economics.

2. On-line colleges have been made possible by the innovation and information management offered by the internet. Whether or not on-line colleges will replace traditional colleges depends if there is something of value in the traditional college setting. Is there something a face-to-face experience with a professor offers that is valued and cannot be duplicated by the on-line setting?

3. A positive externality represents a benefit receive which was not paid for. The market price of a product represents the benefits that a product offers. It also represents the revenue a producer receives for supplying those benefits. So a positive externality represents a benefit received that is not transformed into revenue for the firm. So, one might think that positive externalities might decrease supply.

4. It is set just like it was in the old economy. Firms equate marginal revenue and marginal cost. There is nothing new about this.

5. It depends upon the length of the approval process. The longer the process, the more likely inventors would like the patent period to start at approval in order to give them greater protection time later during the selling period. However, there is a chance that some competitor might come along during the approval period who simply goes ahead and introduces your idea without seeking a patent. Therefore your patent may become worthless while you wait. It seems like there is a double-edged sword here. In general, the longer the period over which economic profits can be earned, the better.

6. It is true that path dependence could implement inefficient technology for a long time. However, if the inefficiency is large and costly to those using it, entrepreneurs would find profit in offering better technology. The fact that some inefficient technology continues to be used suggests that the costliness of the inefficiency is not that great. So new technology would not offer many benefits. This is to say, the added value of a new method might not be very great at all.

7. A patent is a barrier to entry. It allows economic profits to be earned over the patent period. However, this does not mean that others will not try to find their way around the patent, especially if it is very profitable. So by hiring another lawyer to find a way around the patent, my friend is trying to anticipate what the market will do and may be able to develop strategies that will protect the patent's value.

ANSWERS TO CASE STUDY QUESTIONS

Extending the Case Study: Winner Takes All

a. Yes. The purchase of a videotape player indicated that a consumer was dedicated to one of the technologies. When consumers made a purchase, they would find it in their interests to buy the technology that had the greatest likelihood of being the winner. This would preempt the need to buy two machines per TV. As more and more people purchased VHS technology, others would be encouraged to also buy a VHS-based system.

b.   The winner would be the only supplier of that technology. At least for awhile, the winner would be a price-maker with significant powers. Because they would be supplying the entire market ,a new entrant would need to be big right away to have average costs at a competitive level. There would be competition coming from innovation and invention.

c.   DVD technology is replacing VHS. Some major video chains have indicated that they will stop carrying tape movies in the near future and only supply DVDs. This new technology is the competition VHS feared. Barriers to entry do not last forever.

CHAPTER 10

The Firm's Architecture: Organization and Corporate Culture

CHAPTER OVERVIEW

A recurring theme of "The New Managerial Economics" is that managers must make decisions in such a way so as to add value. This was pretty obvious when it was argued that managers must know the customer. It was also obvious when we examined the relationship between production decisions and the behavior of costs. Clearly, managers must understand revenue and costs in order to see their roles in determining economic profit.

In this chapter, the framework of adding value is applied to an area of business where the benefits of using economic analysis may not be so obvious – how a firm is structured. This architecture includes the extent of the value chain, both horizontal and vertical, and how internal relationships are structured. Within this perspective, we also see the importance of transactions costs and the nature of contracts. In each instance, importance is placed on adding efficiency. Lastly, the importance of corporate culture is examined.

KEY CONCEPTS FOR REVIEW

vertical integration	using the market
upstream	downstream
make-or buy-decision	transaction costs
contracts	hostages
buyback	offsets
team	self-managed team
U-form, unitary form, functional form	M-form, multidivisional form
matrix	network
corporate culture	enforceable contracts
hierarchical form	departmentalization
diversification	cash cow
relationship-specific asset	

ACTIVE REVIEW

Completion Questions

1. Organizational structures last over the long run because they are _____.

2. A more efficient organizational structure will lead to _____ profits.

3. As businesses become more complex, single owners often turn to a _____.

4. In the 1990s, there was a tendency to _____ hierarchical structures.

5. The _____ boundaries begin with the acquisition of raw materials and end with the distribution and sale of finished products.

6. When the firm itself carries out the next step in the supply chain rather than relying on the market, the firm is described as _____.

7. One firm's relationship to another is often referred to as being _____ or _____ in the supply chain.

8. A _____ is the managerial decision to perform an upstream or downstream activity internally or to purchase it from an independent firm.

9. Ronald Coase was the first to describe the concept of _____.

10. _____ include all costs involved in an exchange.

11. _____ arise when the costs of exchange are higher without them.

12. _____ and _____ are examples of a hostage situation in contract enforcement.

13. The purpose of an _____ is to compensate the buyer of a good for some of the costs of purchase through other ancillary transactions.

14. In a _____, individuals work together toward a common set of objectives.

15. An organization that has a series of managers and supervisors is referred to as a _____ form.

16. A standard term for a firm having wide horizontal boundaries is _____.

17. _____ exist if the per-unit cost declines as a firm increases the variety of activities it performs or produces.

18. A diversified approach to business structure may help with _____.

19. A business form where a single department is responsible for a single business function is referred to as _____.

20. The _____ structure is a set of autonomous divisions led by a corporate headquarters office.

21. An organizational structure that includes product groups, functional departments, or different types of divisions is called a _____.

22. Over time, the evolution of organizational form has been from _____ to _____.

23. The evolution of organizational form is the result of a _____ process.

24. _____ refers to a set of collectively held beliefs, values, and norms among members of a firm that influences their behaviors and preferences.

25. _____ and _____ do not seem to be closely related.

True-False Questions

1. T F   In the 1990s, the general trend in business organization was toward more hierarchy.

2. T F   Firms must make make-or-buy decisions when considering extending the internal supply chain.

3. T F   When a firm carries out more than one step in the supply chain, the firm is said to be vertically integrated.

4. T F   The relationship of one firm to another in the supply chain is referred to as being aft or starboard.

5. T F   Each step in the supply chain can be viewed as a distinct market.

6. T F   Transaction costs are only present in markets with price makers.

7. T F   Simultaneous exchanges are called spot transactions.

8. T F   Contracts that are enforceable generally do not have penalties.

9. T F   A buyback is the opposite position to an offset.

10. T F   Hostage situations are attempts to enforce contract conditions.

11. T F   Reputation is a means of contract enforcement.

12. T F   Self-managed teams are compensated on the basis of the performance of individuals.

13. T F   Having supervisors reduces the number of individual interactions.

14. T F   Departmentalization can be a grouping based on activity.

15. T F   A very broad horizontal boundary is a diversified firm.

16. T F   Economies of scope are actually economies of scale along the vertical dimension of the supply chain.

17. T F   Diversification can improve cash flow management.

18. T F   Diversification always generates greater returns relative to single product ventures.

19. T F   Diversification always generates growth that is consistent with the preferences of stockholders.

20. T F   U-forms of business create divisions around product lines.

21. T F   Internal structures that generate economic profits will not be imitated due to patent laws.

22. T F   Matrix structures can be built around various groupings, including product and function.

23. T F   MBWA is an orchestra model of hierarchy.

24. T F   Outsourcing tends to flatten an organization.

25. T F   Corporate culture and business performance are closely correlated.

26. T F   Corporate culture can be a low cost form of communication.

Multiple-Choice Questions

1. Institutions, organizations, and organizational structures exist in the long run because they are
    a. government regulated.
    b. generating normal profits.
    c. efficient and adding value.
    d. covering all accounting costs.

2. The 1990s have seen a general trend in organizational structure. This trend is toward
    a. more hierarchy.
    b. flattening.
    c. the U-form of internal structure.
    d. the M-form of internal structure.

3. Enron was structured around
    a. having no fixed assets.
    b. open information.
    c. extensive fixed asset holdings.
    d. who knows what.

4. Firms with a presence along the supply chain are know as
    a. horizontally integrated.
    b. laterally integrated.
    c. merged acquisitions.
    d. vertically integrated.

5. A firm's relationship to another along the supply chain is referred to as being either
    a. back or front.
    b. aft or starboard.
    c. left or right.
    d. upstream or downstream.

6. Each step in the supply chain involves a
   a. make-or-buy decision.
   b. buy-or-sell decision.
   c. buyback-or-offset decision.
   d. a no-go decision.

7. Market exchanges
   a. are zero sum games.
   b. involve transaction costs.
   c. are always forward contracts.
   d. are free.

8. Contracts arise when
   a. transaction costs are zero.
   b. buyers want to exploit sellers.
   c. transactions costs are large.
   d. spot transactions are done over the internet.

9. A buyback is a means of enforcing a contract
   a. in a spot transaction.
   b. when legal enforcement is costly.
   c. when transaction costs are low.
   d. is a Wal-Mart return policy.

10. The purpose of an offset is
    a. to compensate the buyer of a good for some of the costs of purchase through ancillary transactions.
    b. legal only in the EURO currency region.
    c. to replace a buyback in agricultural products.
    d. done in a spot market transaction.

11. Ways to enforce contracts include
    a. buybacks and offsets.
    b. personal reputation.
    c. penalties for breach.
    d. all of the above are used.

12. Lincoln Electric is known
    a. for its use of teams.
    b. for it use of self-managed teams.
    c. for rewarding employees on individual performance.
    d. developing the U-form of organizational structure.

13. The variety of products and services a business offers determines its
    a. vertical boundaries.
    b. horizontal boundaries.
    c. lateral boundaries.
    d. use of offsets in contract enforcement.

14. If per-unit costs decline as a firm increases the variety of activities it performs,
    a. it is experiencing economies of scope.
    b. it is experiencing economies of scale.
    c. it is supplying the entire market for one of the activities.
    d. it is in the range of constant returns to scale.

15. Diversification
    a. reduces growth potential.
    b. enhances cash flow management.
    c. reduces the economies of scope that are available to the firm.
    d. assure above-normal returns to shareholders.

16. The U-form for internal structure is based along
    a. product lines.
    b. matrix intersections.
    c. client lines.
    d. functional lines.

17. If a company wanted to structure its internal operations along product lines, it might favor the
    a. U-form.
    b. matrix alignment.
    c. M-form.
    d. inverse hierarchy.

18. If a company wanted to structure its internal operations along the basic functions of business, it might favor the
    a. U-form
    b. matrix alignment.
    c. M-form.
    d. inverse hierarchy.

19. MBWA stands for
    a. managing by walking around.
    b. managing by winning authority.
    c. managing by wanting attendance.
    d. managing by wondering aloud.

20. Downsizing tends to
    a. extend the supply chain.
    b. flatten the organization.
    c. widen the horizontal boundaries.
    d. extend the vertical reach.

Eliminating middle management
    a. increases the efficiency of upper management.
    b. raises the marginal product of labor.
    c. may increase the workload of upper management.
    d. is generally a good thing to do.

22. Organizational structure is a strategic asset
    a. if it can be copied.
    b. if it assures normal profit.
    c. if it is new.
    d. if it adds value and cannot be copied.

23. Corporate culture can be maintained by
    a. training.
    b. having corporate legends.
    c. honoring younger workers who adopt the culture.
    d. all of the above.

24. Performance and corporate culture
    a. are not closely related.
    b. are closely related.
    c. are inversely related.
    d. are proportional to market share.

Short-Answer Questions

1. What should be the goal of all organizational structures?

2. What has been the general trend in organizational structures over the past 100 years?

3. Differentiate between vertical and horizontal boundaries.

4. What determines the degree to which a firm is vertically integrated?

5. What is a transaction cost?

6. Why are there contracts?

7. Why are hostage situations used?

8. What is a buyback?

9. What is an offset contract?

10. What is departmentalization?

11. When does a firm experience economies of scope?

12. What is the difference between a U-form of internal structure and an M-form structure?

13. According to economic analysis, when does the internal structure change?

14. When are supervisors needed?

15. When can an organizational structure be a strategic asset?

16. What is corporate culture?

17. What is the evidence concerning the relationship between corporate culture and corporate performance?

Applications and Problems

1. Virtually all firms hire labor through the use of implicit or explicit contracts. They usually take the form where a worker agrees to show up at a certain time each day (as well as stating other conditions of employment), and the firm will pay them a certain amount on a certain day. Why is this so common?

2. What is outsourcing and what does it do the organizational structures?

3. What is the difference between structure and culture? Can there be just one structure and just one culture?

4. The corporate form of business has been criticized for not being efficient. This is based on the separation of ownership and daily control. Stockholders, the owners, provide financial capital but do not show up on a day-to-day basis to check on corporate managers. Therefore, managers can misuse stockholder money without apparent consequences. Argue that the corporate form of business with stockholders and managers is efficient.

5. Are corporate takeovers a means to monitor organizational structure and culture?

Extending the Case Study: Culture Clashes

Corporate culture represents the values and practices that are shared across a firm and are passed on from older to younger members of the firm. As the case shows, the merging of two firms and their cultures is difficult and often prevents the attainment of a merger's goals. The power of culture is not just seen in business, however. The current war on terrorism has brought to light the cultures of the FBI, CIA, NSA, and other agencies and the problems they cause with respect to data processing and sharing.

a. Is corporate culture an input or an output?

b. Why is there not one corporate culture?

c. What makes a culture successful? What makes a culture unsuccessful?

d. What is the purpose of a culture in a government agency? What is the goal of a government manager? Could culture in this context be a barrier to entry?

ANSWERS TO ACTIVE REVIEW QUESTIONS

Completion Questions

1. efficient
2. above-normal
3. professional manager
4. flatten
5. vertical
6. vertically integrated
7. upstream, downstream
8. make-or-buy decision
9. transaction cost
10. Transaction cost
11. Contracts

12. Buybacks, offsets
13. offset
14. self-managed team
15. hierarchical
16. diversification
17. Economies of scope
18. cash flow
19. U-form
20. M-form
21. matrix
22. hierarchical, non-hierarchical
23. competitive
24. Corporate culture
25. Corporate culture, performance

True-False Questions

1.	False	2.	True	3.	True
4.	False	5.	True	6.	False
7.	True	8.	False	9.	False
10.	True	11.	True	12.	False
13.	True	14.	True	15.	True
16.	False	17.	True	18.	False
19.	False	20.	False	21.	False
22.	True	23.	True	24.	True
25.	False	26.	True		

Multiple-Choice Questions

1.	c	2.	b	3.	a
4.	d	5.	d	6.	a
7.	b	8.	c	9.	b
10.	a	11.	d	12.	c
13.	b	14.	a	15.	b
16.	d	17.	c	18.	a
19.	a	20.	b	21.	c
22.	d	23.	d	24.	a

Short-Answer Questions

1. The goal of all organizational structures should be to be efficient and to add value.
2. The trend has been toward a less hierarchical form which focuses on core competencies.
3. The vertical boundary of a firm is the extent to which it covers the length of the supply chain. The horizontal boundary of a firm are the varieties of products and services it produces – its scope of products.
4. Firms must make a make-or-buy decision is determining how extended it should be over the supply chain. The more "make" decisions, the more vertically integrated.
5. Transaction costs are all those costs associated with an exchange.
6. Contracts exist because the costs of exchange – the transaction costs – are higher. Contracts are used in place of costly periodic spot transactions.
7. Hostage situations are used when legal enforcement is costly and the gains from trade cannot be attained through spot transactions.
8. Buybacks are like a joint venture. Two organizations provide some inputs to a production process, and the good produced is allocated to the two firms in some pre-arranged way.
9. An offset contract is another hostage situation. In an offset, the seller incurs the obligation to generate an ancillary transaction of a certain value to offset the initial buyer's capital expenditure.
10. Departmentalization is a grouping along dimensions such as a common task, function, product, input, location, etc.
11. Economies of scope are realized if the per-unit cost of output declines as a firm increases the variety of activities it performs.
12. A U-form structure refers to the case where a single department is responsible for a single basic business function. The M-form structure is a set of autonomous divisions led by a corporate headquarters. Rather than along function, an M-form is organized along a product line, a region, a business unit and the like.
13. The internal structure will change when an alternative structures is seen as adding more value than the current form.
14. Supervisors offer value when the work that is being done is less routine and when one cannot rely on learned rules or policies.
15. It can become a strategic asset if it adds value and if it cannot be copied.
16. Corporate culture refers to a set of collectively held beliefs, values, and norms of behavior among members of a firm that influences individual employee preferences and behaviors.
17. The evidence suggests that there is little relationship between the two. This does not mean this it is not important. This simply means that it is not important to sustaining economic profit.

Applications and Problems

1. If labor were not hired in this way, firms would need to hire workers through spot transactions every day and workers would need to find jobs every day. The contract arrangement reduces the cost of the firm hiring workers every day and reduces the costs of workers trying to find jobs every day. The contract reduces transactions costs. It is much more efficient.
2. Outsourcing is where a company hires another firm to perform some function or to produce some product that it used to do or produce itself. Outsourcing usually occurs through the

supply chain. So, outsourcing will tend to flatten organizational structures and allow the contracting business to focus on it core competency.

3. Structure is the formal way resources are related to each other. Culture is the set of norms, values, or rules that arise from individuals interacting within a given structure. Any structure or culture that adds value or economic profit will be copied. So, in a sense, if one is the best, only one would arise. However, there is little evidence that performance and culture are related. Over time, however, firms are moving toward flatter organizations. Therefore, in theory, there may be one structure but many cultures.

4. If this arrangement were not efficient, it would change. The structure of stockholders and managers is not changing substantially, so apparently there are still ways in which managers can be monitored so that they don't waste stockholder money.

5. Certainly. In a takeover bid, the buyer is essentially saying that they can rearrange business resources and add more value than the current arrangement is creating. Thus, takeover activity is found in areas of organization structure that are viewed as being inefficient.

ANSWERS TO CASE STUDY QUESTIONS

Extending the Case Study: Culture Clashes

a. In Chapter 5, "Costs," it was argued that the costs of production can be traced back to how managers arrange inputs, both fixed and variable. This arrangement is guided by the goal to add value. While a manifestation of the arrangements between factors of production is culture, it is probably more important to see that culture is what is used to minimize the costs of communication between inputs. In this context, culture is an input even though it might be initially seen as an output. Ask this a different way. What would management do if the technical arrangements between fixed and variable inputs were not efficient and not adding value? The answer, is that they would change it. Is culture any different? Changing arrangements, whether they are technical or cultural, is costly. But if the marginal benefits are greater than the marginal costs, then new arrangements should be made. The difficulty of culture is probably associated with its measurement.

b. Firms will duplicate those things that add value. Remember, managers are always looking or a way to add value. Those things that do so are copied by others. Given that there is not one to two main cultures suggests that it is not that important to the addition of value.

c. A successful culture is one that adds value while an unsuccessful culture reduces value. The importance of economic profit was seen in Chapters 6 and 7. It was obvious that economic profits are difficult to maintain over the long run. Managers must always be on the lookout for new areas of innovation and the like that allow economic profits to be captured and value to be added. This suggests that whatever the form of corporate culture, it must allow for the changing environment that the search for economic profit entails. An inflexible culture can not survive.

d. The primary purpose of a bureaucratic culture is probably the same as for a profit-seeking corporate culture. It is to minimize transaction costs between resources. Economists argue that the goal of government bureaucrats is to maximize their budgets. One way to do this is to convince Congress, the President, and others that a unique agency is the only agency that can attain a given mission and assignment. For example, the FBI wants to convince budget makers that only the FBI can do what the FBI does. So, it is in the interests of the managers of bureaucracies to prevent others from doing its mission. This is just another way to say, "create a barrier." The more an agency can isolate itself – create a barrier – the better off it might be in getting a larger budget. Unique cultures can isolate. As such, a culture may help limit competition between agencies and, thereby, protect a budget.

CHAPTER 11

Personnel and Compensation

CHAPTER OVERVIEW

A firm is a set of cooperating inputs lead by command. In the last chapter, "The Firm's Architecture: Organizations and Culture," we examined the nature of the organizational structure and culture of the firm. In this context, we looked at the vertical and horizontal boundaries of the firm, its formal internal structure, and the corporate culture that is generated in it. In this chapter, we continue our examination of behavior within the firm. In particular, we examine the relationships between labor inputs and how they interact with each other toward the goal of adding value. While it might make managing easier if everyone was altruistic and totally dedicated to the goals of the firm, it is more the case that individual workers across all areas of production are self-interested. This is to say, they place their own individual interests before all others. Therefore, it is necessary to examine this behavior and how systems of compensation and wages may be used to align individual interests with the interests of the firm. This is also formally developed in the appendix using calculus.

KEY CONCEPTS FOR REVIEW

efficiency wage	backloaded or deferred compensation
wage compression	piecework rates
free-ride	optimal or efficient contracts
golden parachutes	greenmail
poison pill	principal-agent relationship
moral hazard	groupthink
risk-sharing	stock options
corporate governance	tournaments
superstar effect	value of the marginal product
marginal revenue product	

ACTIVE REVIEW

Completion Questions

1. A firm is a set of resources combined to generate value that _____ what each resource alone could produce.

2. Economists describe individual behavior as being _____.

3. When one individual acts on behalf of another, a _____ exits.

4. Employees are _____.

5. One problem with the principal-agent relationship is that interests often do not _____.

6. If an agent does something other than what was agreed to with the principal, then there is a case of _____.

7. The problem of moral hazard often arises when the behavior of an agent or principle is _____.

8. When an employee is paid more than the opportunity cost or more than the market wage, they are being paid an _____.

9. When workers are paid less than what they are worth to the firm early in their tenure and more than what they are worth late in their tenure, the pay structure is referred to as _____.

10. _____ compensation is a means of tying an employee to a firm.

11. A graphical representation of compensation with respect to time, is called a _____.

12. A flat wage profile exhibits _____.

13. Lincoln Electric pays employees on a _____ basis.

14. If individual productivity is difficult to measure, then compensation based on a _____ basis would not be very effective.

15. Team members often have the incentive to _____ on the work of others.

16. _____ is a problem whenever output is team oriented and an individual's contribution to that output is not easily measured.

17. _____ is one way to deal with free-riding in a team setting.

18. _____ evaluations are a means to reduce free-riding.

19. Individuals who are _____ will tend to buy insurance.

20. A _____ often creates an incentive for an employee to contribute to the company beyond the employee's job and also monitor the behavior of other employees.

21. _____ are often used to align the interests of executives with the interests of shareholders.

22. The use of _____ and _____ during the 1980s, made it easier for investors to take over a company.

23. Severance contracts that compensate managers for the loss of their jobs in the event of a change in control of a company are called _____ .

24. The pay of CEOs is significantly greater than many of the other employees of a firm. _____ and _____ have been used to explain the size of the difference.

25. _____ is equal to marginal product multiplied by output price while _____ is equal to marginal product multiplied by marginal revenue.

True-False Questions

1. T F   A firm is a set of resources combined to generate value that exceeds what each resource alone could produce.

2. T F   When someone is hired to pursue the interests of another, there is a principal-agent relationship.

3. T F   Individuals are motivated by rational altruism.

4. T F   Some people argue that compensation schemes can reduce the pride people take in their work.

5. T F   The hired manager is the principal of the owner or owners.

6. T F   There is perfect information between a principal and her agent.

7. T F   Moral hazard is a problem inherent in the principal-agent relationship.

8. T F   An efficiency wage is a wage that is equal to a worker's opportunity cost.

9. T F   Firms pay efficiency wages to keep workers from leaving.

10. T F   Backloaded compensation pays workers less than they are worth in their later years of tenure.

11. T F   Backloaded firms are generally ones that resist downsizing labor.

12. T F   Wage compression results in a steep wage profile.

13. T F   Piecework pay rates are used in a team setting.

14. T F   Piecework pay requires that individual productivity be observed directly.

15. T F   Free-riding in teams can be used to replace groupthink.

16. T F   Free-riding is a problem that cannot be addressed.

17. T F   Subjective evaluations and team member evaluations can be used to control free-riding.

18. T F   Bonuses are a form of risk-sharing.

19. T F   Risk-preferring individuals are ones that always by a lot of insurance.

20. T F   Risk that is beyond the control of a worker does not require a wage premium.

21. T F   A bonus is like an insurance co-payment.

22. T F   The interests of executives are aligned with the interests of shareholders. This is why they are the executives.

23. T F   Stock options can be an effective way to align the interests of the CEO with the interests of shareholders.

24. T F   Monitoring problems are the source of many principal-agent relationship problems.

25. T F   Greenmail is a Dr. Seusse character.

26. T F   Corporate takeovers can serve to monitor executive behavior.

27. T F   Board members may be compensated with stock options.

28. T F   The superstar effect has been used to explain the levels of CEO compensation.

29. T F   Value of the marginal product is equal to marginal product multiplied by marginal revenue.

30. T F   Marginal revenue product is equal to marginal product multiplied by marginal revenue.

Multiple-Choice Questions

1. All the resources that make up a firm
    a. have the exact same interests.
    b. have different interests.
    c. have lateral interests.
    d. are altruistic toward stockholders.

2. Economists describe individual behavior as
    a. rationally altruistic.
    b. rationally self-indulgent.
    c. rationally self-interested.
    d. rationally self-reliant.

3. When one individual acts on behalf of another, there is
    a. always an enforceable contract.
    b. no problem with moral hazard.
    c. a moral commitment.
    d. a principal-agent relationship.

4. Problems associated with a principal-agent relationship include
   a. the matching of interests and moral hazard.
   b. the matching of relationships and moral interests.
   c. monitoring and moral indulgence.
   d. rational self-indulgence.

5. Firms often use an efficiency wage to align the interests of workers with the interests of the firm. This means that
   a. a worker is paid his opportunity cost.
   b. a worker is paid more than his or her opportunity cost.
   c. a worker is paid less than his or her opportunity cost.
   d. a worker is paid the prevailing market wage.

6. When compensation is backloaded
   a. workers are paid their worth in every year.
   b. workers are paid less than their worth in their later years.
   c. workers are paid more than their worth in their later years.
   d. workers are paid more than their worth early in their employment tenure.

7. A heavily backloaded compensation scheme is seen in a
   a. flat wage profile.
   b. wage profile with a slight upward slope.
   c. negatively sloped wage profile.
   d. steep wage profile.

8. When backloaded compensation is used
   a. firms will be quick to lay off workers.
   b. firms will require a buy-in by shareholders.
   c. firms will be reluctant to lay off workers.
   d. firms will remain indifferent about laying off workers.

9. A flat compensation profile reflects
   a. wage compression.
   b. wage leakage.
   c. wage expansion.
   d. wage rollover.

10. Lincoln Electric successfully used what kind of compensation scheme?
    a. wage compression
    b. piecework
    c. stock options
    d. A flat contract rate.

11. A piece rate compensation scheme assumes that individual productivity is
    a. duplicated.
    b. team oriented.
    c. measurable.
    d. compressed.

12. Compensation schemes that use teams must be aware of
    a. equality.
    b. the Lincoln Electric incident.
    c. free ticketing.
    d. free-riding.

13. Free-riding can be addressed by
    a. hiring workers with significant altruistic motives.
    b. having workers take on uncontrollable risk.
    c. monitoring workers in various ways.
    d. lecturing team members on the value of sharing.

14. At times, the use of subjective evaluations will promote
    a. rent-seeking.
    b. free-riding.
    c. wage compression.
    d. shirking.

15. When subjective evaluations are used, it is important to
    a. acknowledge effective rent-seeking.
    b. differentiate between good and bad performers.
    c. use wage compression to motivate older workers.
    d. treat everyone the same.

16. Individuals that buy insurance are generally
    a. risk averse.
    b. risk lovers.
    c. risk neutral.
    d. indifferent toward risk-sharing.

17. Workers will participate in risk-sharing
    a. if they are risk lovers.
    b. if they are paid a piece rate.
    c. if their wages are compressed.
    d. if they are paid for it.

18. A bonus
    a. is a form of a piece rate compensation scheme.
    b. can be used to compress wages.
    c. is a form of risk-sharing.
    d. generally does nothing for motivation.

19. Executive compensation schemes need to address
    a. the matching of interests and moral hazard.
    b. the matching of relationships and moral interests.
    c. monitoring and moral indulgence.
    d. rational self-indulgence.

20. A common form of executive compensation is
    a. wage compression.
    b. a stock option.
    c. a stock rollover.
    d. a straight contract hourly wage.

21. The term used for severance contracts that compensate managers when there is a change in control is called
    a. greenmail.
    b. a poison pill.
    c. wage replacement.
    d. a golden parachute.

22. The board of directors must approve which of the following:
    a. golden parachutes.
    b. greenmail.
    c. poison pills.
    d. All of the above need to be approved.

23. When executives implicitly compete with each other for the next position, they are participating in
    a. greenmail.
    b. a golden parachute.
    c. a tournament.
    d. a superstar setting.

Short-Answer Questions

1. How do economists describe individual behavior?

2. What is a principal-agent relationship?

3. What are two problems associated with a principal-agent relationship?

4. What is the goal of contracts and incentive plans?

5. Why would firms pay efficiency wages?

6. What is backloaded compensation?

7. What is a wage profile?

8. What does it mean if a wage profile is flat?

9. Under what circumstances would a piecework compensation scheme seem appropriate?

10. What is an important concern when teams are used to organize work?

11. What is a way to deal with free-riding?

12. What is risk-sharing?

13. Why would risk-sharing arise in employment considerations?

14. What is the purpose of a bonus?

15. What is the purpose of a stock option?

16. Why would a firm need to create a golden parachute for its CEO?

17. What are some reasons CEO are paid so much relative to other employees?

18. Distinguish between the value of the marginal product and marginal revenue product.

Applications and Problems

1. Some argue that FDIC insurance encourages excessive risk-taking by bank executives who are paid on bank performance. Why?

2. Many classes in college use teams. Teachers find that team performance is better if team-member evaluations of other team members are included in the determination of final grades. Why would this be true?

3. Early in U.S. history lighthouses were produced by profit-seeking businesses. This did not last long, and the government had to take over their management. Why?

4. Explain why a golden parachute clause for a CEO might suppress stock price.

5. What would the effect be of letting stockholders sue boards of directors?

Extending the Case Study: Executive Compensation

One of the topics addressed in the text and in the case is the principal-agent issue. This arises when a principal hires an agent to pursue the interests of the principal. A problem in this relationship is that the principal will generally not be around on a regular basis to assure that the agent does what she says she will do. Under this setting, will the agent seek to fill the interests of the principal or will they seek to fill their own interests? This is to say, a problem in the principal-agent relationship is associated with monitoring. How does a principal assure the compliance of agents?

Day-to-day managers are the agents hired by stockholders (or the board of directors) to pursue the interests of stockholders – to maximize their wealth. The issue of the case is the use of stock options and whether they are effective in achieving this matching of principal and agent interests.

a. Why don't stockholders simply show up and surprise the managers with a visit? Would this be a form of monitoring?

b. Give an example of this mismatch of interests. How might it be seen?

c. Does the amount of stock offered in the stock option matter? How much stock should day-to-day managers be given?

d. Does the time period over which the option can be exercised matter?

ANSWERS TO ACTIVE REVIEW QUESTIONS

Completion Questions

1. exceeds
2. rationally self-interested
3. principal-agent relationship
4. agents
5. align
6. moral hazard
7. difficult to see
8. efficiency wage
9. backloaded
10. Backloaded
11. wage profile

12. wage compression
13. piecework
14. piece work rate
15. free-ride
16. Free riding
17. Peer pressure
18. Subjective
19. risk averse
20. bonus
21. Stock options
22. leveraged buyouts, management buyouts
23. golden parachutes
24. Tournaments, super star effects
25. Value of the marginal product, marginal revenue product

True-False Questions

1.	True	2.	True	3.	False
4.	True	5.	False	6.	False
7.	True	8.	False	9.	True
10.	True	11.	True	12.	False
13.	False	14.	True	15.	False
16.	True	17.	True	18.	True
19.	False	20.	False	21.	True
22.	False	23.	True	24.	True
25.	False	26.	True	27.	True
28.	True	29.	False	30.	True

Multiple-Choice Questions

1.	b	2.	c	3.	d
4.	a	5.	b	6.	c
7.	d	8.	c	9.	a
10.	b	11.	c	12.	d
13.	c	14.	a	15.	b
16.	a	17.	d	18.	c
19.	a	20.	b	21.	d
22.	d	23.	c		

Short-Answer Questions

1. Economists describe the behavior of individuals as being rationally self-interested. In this model, economists believe that individuals consider the costs and the benefits of choices and actions.

2. A principal-agent relationship is one in which an individual acts on the behalf of another. The agent is the party acting on behalf of the other.

3. First, it is not necessarily the case that the interests of the agent and interests of the principal are the same. So, the principal must take steps to align the interests of the agent with their own. The second problem relates to moral hazard. Once the agent has agreed to do certain things for the agent, the agent takes actions that are opposed to the prior agreement.

4. The goals of contracts and incentives is to align the interests of agents with those of principals.

5. An efficiency wage is a wage that is in excess of a worker's opportunity cost or in excess of the market wage. This is paid to impose a cost on a worker for being dismissed from a job. This is an attempt to align the interests of the worker to those of the firm – the principal.

6. This is when a firm pays a worker less than they are worth earlier in their tenure and then pays the worker more than they are worth as their tenure extends. This is paid to encourage a worker to stay with a firm. The longer they stay, the better off they are.

7. A wage profile is the graphical pattern of compensation against time. The resulting line is upward sloping in some way.

8. A flat wage profile is indicative of wage compression. Here, new workers are hired for about the same wage as is being paid to workers with longer tenure.

9. A piecework compensation scheme would be appropriate when a worker's productivity is easily observed and if the firm wanted workers to be treated as individuals rather than to use teams.

10. An important concern is free-riding or shirking. One worker is able to hide his or her individual effort given that the entire team is being judged by the effort of the entire group.

11. One way is to create a system of monitoring within the team. If team members are able to evaluate the efforts of others, then other team members find that there is a cost to their free-riding. Profit-sharing and subjective evaluations are others.

12. Risk-sharing occurs when the aggregate cost of bearing risk is lower when more than one individual shares the risk compared to when each bears the risk individually.

13. Risk-sharing would arise when moral hazard is likely. The firm needs to be certain that the employee does what he or she has agreed to perform. This is true when monitoring individual behavior is costly.

14. A bonus is associated with risk-sharing and attempts to minimize moral hazard.

15. A stock option attempts to align the interests of executives with those of shareholders.

16. If the CEO is risk-averse and if she is worried about job loss, then she would need to be paid a premium to remain in her current job. A golden parachute does just that. It pays the CEO in case they are replaced when the control of a firm changes hands.

17. Some have argued that tournaments explain this wage pattern. Here, workers compete for positions above their own. By offering high pay, the firm is able to elicit hard work from those at lower levels and is better able to identify the most capable. Another explanation is the superstar effect.

18. The value of the marginal product is equal to marginal product multiplied by output price. Marginal revenue product is equal to marginal product multiplied by marginal revenue.

Applications and Problems

1. FDIC insurance guarantees deposits up to a certain amount in case the bank fails. With this insurance, bank managers know that if they take too much risk in order to enhance the profitability of the bank – and thereby enhance their pay – there are no consequences to their failure. Their mistakes is covered by the government. This has also been used by some to argue that Boards of banks don't monitor CEOs closely because they, too, know that insurance is there to cover mistakes. This is a problem of moral hazard.
2. Free-riding is a problem with teams. Given that teams are judged on team performance, then some individuals will shirk and ride on the efforts of others. Member evaluations are a form of monitoring that attempts to address the free-riding problem. Given that monitoring occurs, team members that might otherwise free-ride find it in their interests to make a contribution that is valued by others.
3. Once the light was turned on for one paying customer, other ships that did not pay also benefited from the light. Therefore the lighthouse owner had a free-rider problem. So, lighthouses were not profitable because of free-riding. Given that lighthouse were necessary for trade, the government had to take over their management and use general tax collections to pay for them.
4. A golden parachute is paid to a CEO when there is a takeover by others. One might argue that if the CEO knows that they have such a deal, they might not work as hard to meet the interests of shareholders. If shareholders think in this way, then they might sell their shares. This would suppress stock price, ceteris paribus.
5. Boards might be more attentive to the interests of stockholders. This might include better monitoring of executives.

ANSWERS TO CASE STUDY QUESTIONS

Extending the Case Study: Executive Compensation

a. Showing up with a surprise visit would be a form of monitoring but probably not a very effective one. Does the stockholder have sufficient knowledge to judge the behavior of managers? Also, if one stockholder showed up, other stockholders would free-ride on their behavior. Stockholders have alternative uses for their time, so visiting a corporation would offer little in benefit and could be costly. Also, stockholders generally have diversified portfolios. As such, they hold stock across many companies and not enough of one to make it in their interests to show up. All they are interested in is that their stock shares are accurately priced.
b. An example might be that a stockholder invests one dollar in a company. She expects that managers will use that dollar to create added value. However, given that the stockholder is not going to show up, the manager takes that dollar and uses it for himself. For example, he might buy real art for his office rather than prints. The art makes the manager better off but did not create added value for the stockholder.
c. Yes, it probably does. Take the example in answer b. Assume that the manager is given ten percent of the stock. So, with one dollar in stockholder wealth, the manager looses out of ten cents by not creating added value. The manager would still would rather have real art. However, as the percentage rises, the use of the dollar for art has a bigger negative consequence for the manager. So, the marginal benefit of providing an additional option

should be compared to the marginal cost.

d. If the stock option can be exercised next week, managers are given the incentive to do things that will inflate the stock price over the next week. Misreporting information might do this. However, if the option cannot be exercised for five years, managers have the incentive to think about the long term value of the company. This longer view might enhance the creation of added value to a greater degree when compared to a shorter period.

CHAPTER 12

Capital Allocation: Real Options

CHAPTER OVERVIEW

A business firm is one of many organizations that converts inputs into outputs. The overall goal of this endeavor is to add value. In Chapter 11, we examined the role of labor and compensation schemes in the attainment of this end. In this chapter, the role of capital in this process is investigated. Capital expenditures often represent significant outlays of an enterprise's financial resources. It is also the case that capital inputs have useful lives extending beyond the current budget year. Therefore, capital expenditures made today not only represent initial current year spending, but they also represent future spending and future revenues. This has led to the use of capital budgeting to make decisions regarding the use of capital. Yet, for several reasons, this traditional approach leaves a lot to be desired. A new, more flexible approach needs to be used to examine the role of capital resources in the firm. It is in this light that the concept of real options is developed. The real options approach recognizes that changing capital resources is a sequential process and that the contribution of capital to the goal of adding value needs to be considered in more than the "now or never" context of traditional capital budgeting. The use of real options by managers is the focus of this chapter.

KEY CONCEPTS FOR REVIEW

capital budgeting

options

real options

"now or never" decision

net present value, NPV

call and put options

Black-Scholes option pricing formula

ACTIVE REVIEW

Completion Questions

1. _____ is the name given to the traditional comparison of the costs of additional _____ to the additional value it creates.

2. For a capital project to be added, the _____ of the project must be greater than zero.

132 Chapter 12

3. One of the problems with the practice of traditional capital budgeting is that only _____ costs are used rather than _____.

4. The conversion of future dollars into present dollars is called _____.

5. Often, firms have the wrong _____ when making capital budgeting decisions.

6. The use of the _____ as an objective better aligns the capital budgeting process with other incentives within the enterprise.

7. Allocating _____ may be the most crucial aspect of business.

8. In financial terms, an "opportunity" is the same as an _____.

9. With an _____, you have the right, not the _____, to buy or sell something at a specified price on or before some future date.

10. A _____ gives you the right to buy something at a specified price on or before some future date.

11. A _____ is the right to purchase capital or make an investment at some point in the future.

12. An option's value depends on the _____ of the underlying _____, _____, and _____.

13. The _____ attempts to value an option.

14. A project can have a _____ net present value and yet still have value as an option.

15. If the likelihood that the value of an asset will _____ is large, or the time until the final decision has to be made is _____, an option will have value.

16. As the "now or never" decision date nears, the value of an the option will approach the _____ or _____ , whichever is larger.

17. Increased _____ will serve to increase the value of an option.

18. Option analysis indicates that the high value of dot.com stocks in recent years was the result of _____.

19. An option is an _____.

True-False Questions

1. T F   Net present value is central to traditional capital budgeting.

2. T F   Discounting is part of calculating net present value.

3. T F   Traditional capital budgeting is not focused around a "now or never" date.

4. T F   Capital budgeting usually includes only accounting costs.

5. T F   The proper goal for capital budgeting decisions is to maximize the return on assets.

Copyright © South-Western, Cengage Learning. All rights reserved.

6. T   F   Economic profit considerations are not included in capital budgeting decisions.

7. T   F   An option is a right to buy something at a specified price at some point in the future.

8. T   F   An option is an opportunity and an obligation.

9. T   F   A call option is a right to buy while a put option is the right to sell.

10. T   F   An investment opportunity has option characteristics.

11. T   F   Real option analysis applies options theory to capital acquisitions.

12. T   F   The Black-Scholes pricing model prices the net present value of a project at a unique point of time.

13. T   F   The project's volatility is not used in the pricing of an option.

14. T   F   The value of an option varies with the volatility of the project.

15. T   F   The time period of the option affects the value of the option.

16. T   F   Options analysis suggests that the shares of dot.com ventures were accurately priced.

17. T   F   As the "now or never" date approaches, the option price tends to zero or the net present value, whichever is greater.

18. T   F   It is not possible to have a negative net present value and a positive options price.

Multiple-Choice Questions

1. The traditional model for making capital acquisitions is called
    a. capital budgeting.
    b. capital allocation.
    c. Black-Scholes pricing.
    d. real options analysis.

2. Under traditional capital budgeting a capital project is acceptable if
    a. its discounted value of added revenue is greater than zero.
    b. its options price is greater than one.
    c. the net present value is greater than zero.
    d. the net present value is negative.

3. To an economist, the goal of business should be to
    a. maximize sales.
    b. maximize economic profits.
    c. maximize accounting profits.
    d. maximize the return on assets.

4. A call option is the
    a. right to sell something.
    b. right to price something.
    c. obligation to buy something.
    d. right to buy something.

5. Option analysis is built around the idea that capital acquisition decisions
    a. are made with perfect information.
    b. are made in a series of steps.
    c. are made at one, and only one, point in time.
    d. are based on net present value calculations.

6. An option
    a. does not need to be in the money all the time.
    b. needs to be in the money all the time.
    c. is not sold unless it is in the money.
    d. is a requirement to buy.

7. A real option
    a. is a stock option.
    b. is the right to sell capital.
    c. is the right to buy capital.
    d. is the obligation to buy capital.

8. To use the Black-Scholes pricing model, you need to know
    a. the value of the project.
    b. the cost to exercise the option and the time it expires.
    c. the risk-free rate.
    d. project volatility.
    e. All of the above are required.

9. What does a dollar amount for a real option tell you?
    a. It tells you the future value of future events.
    b. It tells you the value today of a future opportunity.
    c. It tells you the value today of an opportunity today.
    d. It tells you the net present value of a "now or never" decision.

10. Real options analysis indicates that the recent valuation of dot.com stocks was
    a. representative of real opportunities.
    b. low and that buying recommendations were reasonable.
    c. a mystery.
    d. excessive.

11. Which of the following will raise the value of a real option?
    a. higher volatility.
    b. lower volatility.
    c. shorter duration.
    d. higher costs.

12. Which of the following will reduce the value of a real option?
    a. A higher volatility.
    b. A longer time until the option must be exercised.
    c. A shorter time until the option must be exercised.
    d. Lower costs associated with the project.

Short-Answer Questions

1. What is capital budgeting?

2. Under the traditional capital budgeting paradigm, when is a new capital project accepted?

3. What are some problems with traditional capital budgeting?

4. Why does net present value not always equal the discounted value of economic profit?

5. What is an option?

6. What is the difference between and put and a call?

7. What is a real option?

8. What is unique about the real options approach to capital acquisitions?

9. What determines the value of an option?

10. Why is a corporate opportunity like an option?

11. What does the Black-Scholes model do?

12. What data do you need to be able to use the Black-Scholes pricing model?

13. Why is uncertainty valued in option analysis?

14. Why can a project have a negative net present value but a positive option value?

15. As the "now or never" date approaches, what does the option value do?

Applications and Problems

1. Assume that the net present value of some project is zero. However, the real option value on the same project is greater than zero. Why can this happen? What is the option doing?

2. An option may be viewed as an opportunity. It may also be seen as a bet. Assume you buy a call on a stock. What are you doing and what are you betting on? What bet is the seller of the call making?

3. It has been argued in the text that markets process information. What information is the pricing of a real option processing?

4. The text presents the Black-Scholes pricing model. There are other models that price options. What leads to the development of alternative pricing models?

Extending the Case Study: Merck and Medco

This case shows that changes in capital expenditures should be viewed as a series of sequential steps and not just a single one that commits extensive corporate resources to a project that has a multi-year life. Under traditional capital budgeting, the Merck acquisition of Medco would have considered the action's net present value. This views the acquisition as a "now or never" decision at the time of calculation – either Merck buys now or it never does. However, in reality, the acquisition process could have been seen as a series of steps. This is not to say that there is no "now or never" decision. There will be. It will just be in the future at some point. Until that point is reached, Merck could have made a series of smaller expenditures and progressively evaluated their ultimate "now or never" decision. This is what a real option allows you to do – evaluate what the value today is of a future "now or never" decision. With each passing day, new information can be added to the process so that the likelihood would be greater that the final large capital outlay adds value to the overall enterprise.

a. Often, contracts in sports represent a series of years that culminate in a option year. This is in the form of a call option. After the option year, another long-term contract can be negotiated. Is this similar to what a real option approach would have done for Merck? What determines the value of having the option? Frame you answer around a baseball context.

b. Why would a player sign a contract that contains a call option for the team? Isn't an option just that—an option and not an obligation? When would the team exercise the option year?

c. Why would a team sign a contract with an option?

ANSWERS TO ACTIVE REVIEW QUESTIONS

Completion Questions

1. Capital budgeting, capital
2. net present value
3. accounting, total opportunity costs
4. discounting
5. objective
6. discounted value of economic profit
7. capital
8. option
9. option, obligation
10. call option
11. real option
12. value, asset, time, risk
13. Black-Scholes pricing formula
14. negative
15. rise, long
16. net present value, zero
17. volatility
18. over inflated expectations
19. opportunity

True-False Questions

1.	True	2.	True	3.	False
4.	True	5.	False	6.	False
7.	True	8.	False	9.	True
10.	True	11.	True	12.	False
13.	False	14.	True	15.	True
16.	False	17.	True	18.	False

Multiple-Choice Questions

1.	a	2.	c	3.	b
4.	d	5.	b	6.	a
7.	c	8.	e	9.	b
10.	d	11.	a	12.	c

Short-Answer Questions

1. Capital budgeting is the name given to the process of comparing the cost of a capital resource with the additional value it creates.
2. A new capital project is accepted when the present value of the expected cash flows from the project is greater than the present value of the investment's cost. The net present value is greater than zero.
3. Often only accounting costs are used. Also, it is easy to manipulate cash flows to change the net present value to get a favorable decision. Finally, traditional capital budgeting is framed as a "now or never" decision.
4. Net present value calculations usually only consider accounting costs and not all opportunity costs.
5. An option is the right to buy or sell something at a specified price on or before some unique date. In general, an option is an opportunity and not an obligation.
6. A put is the right to sell something while a call is the right to buy something.
7. A real option is the right to purchase capital or make an investment at some point in the future.
8. Real option analysis recognizes that a capital acquisition is not just a "now or never" decision. Rather capital acquisition represents a series of sequential steps that can be managed.
9. The value of an option is determined by the value of the underlying asset, time, and risk.
10. A corporate opportunity is like an option in that when a firm makes an initial investment, it is paying an entry fee, but is not obligated, to continue investing in the future.
11. The Black-Scholes model is used to price options.

12. You need to know the present value of the project, the costs to exercise the option, the risk-free rate, the time to expiration of the option, and project volatility.
13. Uncertainty widens the value of possible outcomes and, thereby, raises the value of the option.
14. The option value depends on uncertainty and the time until the drop-dead date. The higher the volatility and the longer the time until the final decision, the greater will be the value of the option.
15. The option value either approaches the net present value or zero, whichever is greater

Applications and Problems

1. The net present value is based on current estimates of costs and added value. It assumes that a decision on the entire project, including its total funding must be made now. An option is attempting to include in the valuation unseen future expectations and events. Thus, an option might assume an increase in demand for the final product thereby increasing the added value of the project. Traditional capital budgeting and net present value do not offer an easy way to introduce future concepts and changes in their probability of occurring. The option is forcing decision makers to think about the future as well as their ability to affect it.
2. A call is the right to buy something at a specified price by a certain time. In the case of the stock, a call gives the holder of the call the right to buy a certain number of shares at a certain price within a specified time. You are betting that the stock will rise above the price set in the call. In the case that the share price rises above the call, you may buy at the lower price set in the call and then sell at the higher market price. The seller of the call is betting that the price will not rise above the call price. If that is the case, the seller has made money by selling you the call.
3. The pricing of the option is an estimate of the future value of unforeseen events. A call is just one way to put opinions about the future into the market process.
4. One way to judge economic models is whether or not they add value to decision making. Are your decisions better with them compared to decision without using them? Assume that you used the Black-Scholes model to price a real option. At the "now or never" date, the Black-Scholes model converged to the net present value and you decided to go forward with the project. What would happen if you discovered that you made a mistake and that the project would not be profitable? If you were not fired, you would probably review the decision making process, including the Black-Scholes model. Was something left out? You might even look for alternative pricing models to see what they would have said. Economic theory is useful, but it is not perfect. So mistakes and errors promote the development of new models, including option pricing models.

ANSWERS TO CASE STUDY QUESTIONS

Extending the Case Study: Merck and Medco

a. Let's assume we are talking about a three-year contract where the third year is an option year. This means that the team has the right to unilaterally sign the player to the third year at an agreed to price. The team will evaluate the player over the first two years and decide whether or not to exercise its option – the right to sign the player to the third year. The value of this option is dependent on how well the player does in the first two years. This process is similar to what Merck should have done. Few players are signed to extensive multi-year contracts. Most times, team sign contracts of limited duration and watch performances in the interim. The option year offers the team flexibility.

b.   A player signs a contract with an option because he is also uncertain over his future value. He may anticipate bad or average years so that his future value in the market will not be too different than what it is today. The option may give a bit of security. However, the option is at the team's discretion. If the player has career years, then his market value will rise significantly, and the team will certainly exercise or execute the option making the player worse off. Accordingly, when a contract has an option year, players are paid money up front to encourage them to sign a contract that might make them worse off in the future. This payment is called an option premium.

c.   A team wants an option because it is uncertain over the future value of the player. If the player has super years for the first two, the team is better off having the option. It will be able to sign the player to a contract at a wage that was agreed to in the past and that will also probably be less than the market wage in the third year.

CHAPTER 13

Strategic Behavior: The Theory of Games

CHAPTER OVERVIEW

Uncertainty is a constant in business. It may, in fact, be one of those things that makes business exciting. Another constant in business is that decisions never stand alone. Interdependence in decision making is something that every manager must deal with. While the cases in the text tend to stress interdependence between competitors in the product market, managers must also realize that changing employee compensation also has interdependent features, especially if a union is present. Interdependence also exists in capital acquisitions especially if there are other suitors involved. This is to say, there are probably few decisions a manager makes that do not have some aspect of interdependence.

This chapter presents the various ways economists model interdependence and how they may be applied to various business settings. It begins with the simple model of a sequential game where the payoffs are known and ends with a discussion of the assignment of probabilities to uncertain payoffs, outcomes, and responses. All games have common features, but each also has its own unique twist. This is to say, effective management in dynamic and uncertain markets must recognize this interdependence. An understanding of game theory can offer a framework for decision making in this setting.

KEY CONCEPTS FOR REVIEW

game theory

simultaneous game

dominated strategy

prisoner's dilemma

repeated trials

scorched earth policy

expected value

convention

boundaries

sequential game

dominant strategy

Nash equilibrium

commitment

tit-for-tat

risk

risk aversion

rules

end-of-game problem

ACTIVE REVIEW

Completion Questions

1. _____ attempts to model strategic behavior.

2. In a _____ players maker alternating moves.

3. When all players maker moves at the same time without necessarily viewing the moves of others, the game is referred to as _____.

4. In a sequential game, each player must _____ and then _____.

5. If a player has a strategy where one course of action outperforms all others regardless of the moves of other players, then the initial players has a _____.

6. A _____ is uniformly worse than some other strategy. These are avoided whenever possible.

7. Often, when dominated strategies are eliminated, a problem of _____ arises, which suggests the absence of an _____.

8. A _____ exists when no player wants to change their strategy given what the other players are doing.

9. One way to deal with multiple equilibriums is to adopt a _____.

10. A game consists of _____, _____, _____, and _____.

11. To be a successful player in a game, you must be able to offer _____ that cannot be _____.

12. Rules of a game are often the result of _____ action.

13. All players of a game are assumed to be _____.

14. The _____ of the game are often dictated by the size of the _____.

15. A _____ results in an outcome where all parties are worse off than would be the case if the parties could agree to another set of behaviors.

16. _____ and _____ are two ways out of a prisoner's dilemma.

17. A _____ is an action that ties one party into an action and other parties know this is the behavior that will result.

18. A _____ is a form of a commitment as is _____.

19. The _____ and _____ policies are two ways to penalize rivals that do not cooperate.

20. The _____ of an outcome is the probability that it will occur multiplied by its payoff.

True-False Questions

1. T F   Strategic behavior recognizes that actions are interdependent.

2. T F   Game theory attempts of model strategic behavior.

3. T F   A simultaneous game is one where the players make alternating moves.

4. T F   "Look ahead, reason back" is generally associated with a simultaneous game.

5. T F   In a simultaneous game, a player does not have the benefit of knowing a rival's moves before making her own.

6. T F   A dominant strategy is one where my move depends on the moves of a rival.

7. T F   Dominant strategies should be avoided at all costs.

8. T F   Dominated strategies should be avoided at all costs.

9. T F   Circular reasoning can be avoided once all dominated strategies have been eliminated.

10. T F   Sun Country Airlines could have benefited by using real options.

11. T F   Nash equilibriums are unstable.

12. T F   It is possible to have more than one Nash equilibrium.

13. T F   Conventions are used to avoid problems associated with multiple equilibria.

14. T F   Successful players do not really need to consider value added in making their initial decision to play the game.

15. T F   One's value in a game can depend on the number of players in the game.

16. T F   Apple successfully changed the rules of the game.

17. T F   Game theory is not based on the assumption of the rationality of players.

18. T F   If players are rational, they do not make mistakes.

19. T F   A prisoner's dilemma is not efficient.

20. T F   Parties in a prisoner's dilemma can be made better of through the use of credible commitments.

21. T F   Advertising is a variable cost.

22. T F   Repeated transactions do not afford learning.

23. T F   Knowing that the end of the game is nearing will affect actions taken by the players.

24. T F   "Do unto others as they have done unto you" is an example of a scorched earth policy.

25. T F   Tit-for-tat is a way to penalize a player.

26. T F   A strategic move can preempt the moves of others.

27. T F   Game payoffs are certain.

28. T F   Risk averse players will take on risk if they are paid a risk premium.

Multiple-Choice Questions

1. Game theory attempts to model
    a. capital budgeting.
    b. strategic behavior.
    c. real options.
    d. consumer behavior.

2. Games with alternating plays are called
    a. simultaneous games.
    b. real games.
    c. sequential games.
    d. budgeting games.

3. "Look forward, reason back" is associated with what type of game?
    a. A sequential game.
    b. A real game.
    c. A simultaneous game.
    d. A budget game.

4. In a simultaneous game
    a. one has alternating moves.
    b. one can look forward and reason back.
    c. one can benefit by observing the moves of others.
    d. neither player has the benefit of observing the other's complete move before making her own.

5. A strategy that is the best for one party regardless of the strategy of another is a
    a. dominated strategy.
    b. smart strategy.
    c. dominant strategy.
    d. real option.

6. What kind of strategy is uniformly worse than other strategies?
    a. A dominated strategy.
    b. A dominant strategy.
    c. A real strategy.
    d. A Nash equilibrium.

7. A Nash equilibrium exits
    a. when everyone has a dominated strategy.
    b. when strategies are dominant to probabilities.
    c. when there is a combination of strategies in which each player's actions is the best response to the actions of others.
    d. when firms exit the market.

8. The value of a game can be affected by
   a. the number of players in the game.
   b. the value added a player brings to the game.
   c. the rules of the game.
   d. all the above affect the value of the game.

9. The rules of the game
   a. are invariant.
   b. can be influenced by government.
   c. are written documents that are enforceable by law.
   d. are never informal.

10. A prisoner's dilemma
    a. is efficient.
    b. is the outcome where everyone has a dominant strategy.
    c. is inefficient.
    d. causes circular reasoning.

11. A commitment is
    a. an action that ties someone into a certain behavior and others know this is the behavior that will result.
    b. a promise that is legally enforceable.
    c. a rule of the game.
    d. the outcome of a dominated strategy.

12. Examples of a commitment include
    a. guarantees and dominant strategies.
    b. guarantees and real options.
    c. guarantees and barriers to entry.
    d. guarantees and advertising.

13. Repeated transactions
    a. result from a dominant strategy.
    b. do not affect leaning by customers.
    c. will not affect the rules of the game.
    d. represent a way out of a prisoner's dilemma.

14. When the end of the game is near
    a. strategies will change.
    b. strategies will be unaffected.
    c. the rules of the game will be dominated by other strategies.
    d. none of the above are true.

15. If a rival needs to be penalized
    a. government action is required.
    b. a real option should be exercised.
    c. a tit-for-tat strategy may be appropriate.
    d. a dominated strategy is the best action.

16. A scorched earth policy can be viewed as
    a. a real option.
    b. a strategic move.
    c. a dominated strategy.
    d. a game rollover.

17. Game payoffs are
    a. known by all and are certain.
    b. invariant to the rules of the game.
    c. uncertain.
    d. never related to the expected value of the game.

18. Risk averse people will take on risk with the payment of a
    a. real option.
    b. few dollars.
    c. risk option.
    d. risk premium.

19. Cooperation between parties can result from
    a. repeat transactions.
    b. dominant strategies.
    c. dominated strategies.
    d. simultaneous games.

20. Uncertainty can be introduced into a game by
    a. rolling commitments into rules.
    b. assigning probabilities to payoffs.
    c. reducing risk.
    d. making one player follow a dominated strategy.

Short-Answer Questions

1. What is strategic behavior?

2. What is the difference between a sequential game and a simultaneous game?

3. What does it mean to "look forward and reason back?"

4. If player A has a dominant strategy, what will A do when B changes strategy?

5. What is a dominated strategy?

6. What is the nature of a Nash equilibrium?

7. Why do conventions arise?

8. What are the features of a game?

9. To be successful in the market game, what does a player need to possess?

10. What does it mean that the players of a game are rational?

11. Why is a prisoner's dilemma inefficient?

12. What is a commitment?

13. Why do parties want to solve a prisoner's dilemma and how do they do so?

14. What do repeated transactions do?

15. What is the purpose of a tit-for-tat strategy?

16. What is a preemptive strike?

Applications and Problems

1. Executive compensation was discussed in the last chapter. After reading about game theory, could you argue that CEOs are paid a lot for their "experience?" What would this mean?

2. Assume that your rival has a dominant strategy to not advertise. While your most effective strategy is to advertise, your payoff would be greater if your rival would also advertise. What strategy could you develop to alter your rival's payoff in order to make it in her interests to advertise?

3. Colleges often use new majors to gain a competitive strategy. Is this an effective use of a college's resource?

4. People who work for the U.S. Department of Defense claim that some contractors do not initially negotiate in good faith. When bidding on a contract, bidders low-ball, and their bids do not represent their costs of production. However, once they get a contract, they want to renegotiate, claiming that they lose money at the original bid. Why do they follow this strategy?

5. The colleges in the Ivy League used to get together to discuss the ways they award financial aid. Why?

6. Why is a guarantee a commitment?

7. In the text, an example of a movie crash scene was used as an example of a commitment. In it, one driver throws their steering wheel out of the car. The other driver knows what will happen if they don't steer differently. What would happen if it was a simultaneous game and both drivers tossed their steering wheels out of their cars at the same time?

8. Economists have always had a hard time creating models that describe strategic behavior. Why do you think this is the case?

Extending the Case Study: Unilever and P&G

Unilever and P&G, while competitors, appear to have developed a relationship in the market where the strategy of one is relatively apparent to other. This is to say, they have created a semi-certain environment in an uncertain world. Now, Unilever wonders about changing the relationships that has developed out of a series repeat games in what was once a prisoner's dilemma. The context is the introduction of a new product.

a. What is one of the first questions that must be addressed in some way before a new product is introduced?

b. In a game setting, is the answer to question a. changed in anyway?

c. What is the fundamental question that Unilever must answer? Is it really whether or not to introduce a new product in a new way?

d. What is something else that might alter the way both P&G and Unilever introduce new products?

ANSWERS TO ACTIVE REVIEW QUESTIONS

Completion Questions

1. Game theory
2. sequential game
3. simultaneous
4. look forward, reason back
5. dominant strategy
6. dominated strategy
7. circular reasoning, equilibrium
8. Nash equilibrium
9. convention
10. players, players' perceptions, rules, boundaries
11. value added, copied
12. governmental
13. rational
14. boundaries, market
15. prisoner's dilemma
16. commitments, repeated trials
17. commitment
18. guarantees, advertising
19. tit-for-tat, scorched earth
20. expected value

True-False Questions

1.	True	2.	True	3.	False
4.	False	5.	True	6.	False
7.	False	8.	True	9.	False
10.	True	11.	False	12.	True
13.	True	14.	False	15.	True
16.	False	17.	False	18.	False
19.	True	20.	True	21.	False
22.	False	23.	True	24.	False
25.	True	26.	True	27.	False
28.	True				

Multiple-Choice Questions

1.	b	2.	c	3.	a
4.	d	5.	a	6.	a
7.	c	8.	d	9.	b
10.	c	11.	a	12.	d
13.	d	14.	a	15.	c
16.	b	17.	c	18.	d
19.	a	20.	b		

Short-Answer Questions

1. Strategic behavior results when decisions between rivals are interdependent – what one does is affected and affects what others will do.

2. In a sequential game, players make alternating moves. It is possible to look forward and reason back. In a simultaneous game, all players make moves at the same time and each player cannot benefit from seeing what other players did. In this type of game, one can find a prisoner's dilemma.

3. This is the process in a sequential game. You look into the future and attempt to figure out how a rival might act if you take a particular course of action. Then you take this back to the present and hopefully make an effective decision.

4. A dominant strategy is one which is best for a player regardless of what any other player might do. Therefore, A will not change strategy.

5. A dominated strategy is one that is not best for a player of a game.

6. A Nash equilibrium exists when no player wants to change strategies given what other players are doing. There is a combination of strategies in which each player's actions is the best response to the actions of the other parties.

7. There are times when a game may have multiple equilibria. In a sense, there is no unique solution. As such, the problem can be solved by some rule – a convention – that is used when these situations arise.

8. The features of a game include the players, the perceptions of each of the players, the rules of the game, and boundaries to the game.

9. Players must be able to show that they add value. In addition, this ability to add value cannot be easily copied.

10. This means that people do the best that they can, given how they perceive the game and how they evaluate the various possible outcomes of the game. It does not mean that no one makes a mistake.

11. A prisoner's dilemma is where all parties are worse off than would be the case if the parties could agree to another set of behaviors. Since it does have a less than the best outcome, it is inefficient.

12. A commitment is an action that ties one party into a certain behavior and that other parties know that this is the behavior that will result.

13. A prisoner's dilemma is not efficient. By moving from it, it is possible that all parties involved can be better off. Commitments and repeated transactions are ways out of prisoner dilemmas.
14. Repeat transactions allow the parties involved in the game to learn about each other.
15. This is a way to penalize a rival that does not cooperate. I will do to you what you have done to me.
16. A preemptive strike occurs when one party takes an action to force some other action out of another party.

Applications and Problems

1. Throughout this chapter, values have been given by the author to the various payoffs in each of the games. In addition, in the section on uncertainty, probability weights were provide to you. Who determines these outside of the book? Who estimates a payoff and whether or not it is reasonable? Who assigns probability weights that are reasonable and realistic so that expected value calculations are reasonably accurate? If game theory is to enhance decision making, then decision makers must have confidence in the payoffs and probabilities that have been assigned to the various outcomes. Ultimately, it is the chief executive (or her associates) that make and judge the assignments. While analysis can provide numbers, only experience can judge whether or not a number makes sense and is reasonable. Thus, experience is necessary in order to make data useful. This skill has value and is probably worth a great deal in that not everyone can do it.
2. You probably need to alter her perceptions concerning the value of advertising. For example, your advertisements could make product comparisons making your rival's product appear inferior or too expensive. If your campaign were successful, your rival would need to advertise for defensive reasons. As such, your advertisements are of more value once they commence.
3. Majors are probably not a strategic asset. They are easily copied so they offer little value added.
4. The low-ball strategy works because it is an effective way to get contracts. They are following the rules of the game. The Department of Defense will renegotiate because they do not want to have to incur the expense of a complete bidding process. They are saying that the first bidding process is the end of the game. Contractors are simply being rational given the rules of the game. Different rules would elicit different behavior.
5. They are trying to develop cooperation. They all want the best students, and financial aid is one of their recruitment tools. If they did not cooperate, their financial aid awards would probably be bigger and their profits smaller. They are trying to a develop commitment from each other so they can avoid a prisoner's dilemma.
6. A guarantee states that a given behavior will occur if certain things happen in the future. It removes uncertainty for the customer, especially ones that are risk averse.
7. They would crash. This is not rocket science! It would also be a commitment, however. By a present act, a future course is known with certainty.
8. Equilibrium analysis is central to all economic models. Throughout the text, we have seen how the MR=MC rule determines how much a firm will produce. If the firm is not at this level, it will move toward it. This is the nature of an equilibrium. In strategic behavior, however, what I do depends, in part, on what you do and vice versa. When I change, you change, but when you change, I change again. So, it is hard to use an equilibrium framework when the possibility of circular reasoning is likely.

ANSWERS TO CASE STUDY QUESTIONS

Extending the Case Study: Unilever and P&G

a. The first question the introduction of a new product must address is does it add value? This must be answered first if limited business resources are to be used in its development, production, and marketing. A related question is whether the added value the product brings to the market is easily copied by others.

b. In a game setting, the introduction of a new product must answer the first question, but it must also consider whether the new product will also affect the value added by other products. Unilever must not only think about its new product and P&G's response to it; Unilever must also consider if P&G may change their behavior with respect to other products that Unilever offers to consumers. If P&G does not have a new product to offer in competition, will it change its approach to other products in other segments of the market?

c. The fundamental question is, does the new product bring the Unilever and P&G relationship back to one of a prisoner's dilemma. Would a return to this inefficient game setting make Unilever better off relative to maintaining the current state of affairs?

d. The entry of others could also change the relationship that Unilever and P&G have developed. If their relationship is adding value for both, then a competitor will enter the market. Their game setting gets more complicated if this happens.

CHAPTER 14

Globalization

CHAPTER OVERVIEW

Globalization refers to cross border activities as well as borderless transactions; the location of manufacturing facilities in more than one country; the sales of goods and services in several nations; and the acquisition of resources from many nations. These issues face nearly every manager at virtually every level in one way or another. To make effective decisions, managers must be aware of the various ways global issues impact their company. These effects can be felt through balance sheet exposure or through market exposure. While these exposures can be managed to a degree through various types of hedging vehicles, they still represent a source of uncertainty and risk. To begin, one must understand the nature of the foreign exchange market and how exchange rates are determined. Next, market tools like forward and future contracts, and options need to be considered as ways to manage this exposure. Finally, it is important to see that the global capital market is one of the most competitive markets in the world. Capital, to a large degree, is free today to seek its highest valued use. Yet governments still attempt to influence trade and capital flows.

KEY CONCEPTS FOR REVIEW

foreign exchange	exchange rate
forward market	spot market
forward rate	the law of one price
arbitrage	purchasing power parity, PPP
interest rate parity, IRP	balance sheet exposure
market-based exposure	hedging
forwards	currency futures
options	tariffs
quotas	dollarization
appreciation	depreciation
emerging markets	

ACTIVE REVIEW

Completion Questions

1. _____ refers to cross border activities and borderless transaction; the location of manufacturing facilities in more than one country; the sales of goods and services in several nations; and the acquisition of resources from many countries.

2. Foreign money and _____ are synonyms.

3. An _____ is the price of one country's currency in terms of another.

4. The _____ rate is the exchange rate at any point in time.

5. The equilibrium exchange is determined where the _____ equals the _____ .

6. The _____ for a foreign currency is the same as the _____ of the domestic currency.

7. Under a system of _____ , exchange rates are determined by law.

8. A practice where a country replaces its own legal tender with the dollar is called _____ .

9. The _____ argues that identical goods should sell for the same price in different locations except for transportation and transactions costs.

10. The law of one price is formally presented in the concept of _____ .

11. The simultaneous buying in one market and selling in another is called _____ .

12. People engage in arbitrage to take advantage of _____ .

13. When you are subject to changes in exchange rates, we say you are exposed to _____ .

14. _____ is the idea that the rate of return or interest rate will be the same on identical assets when returns are measured in the domestic currency.

15. A firm's _____ is the amount or value at risk.

16. The two primary ways a firm is subject to exchange rate risk is through _____ and through _____ .

17. The _____ allows firms to establish the exchange rate between two currencies for settlement at a fixed future date.

18. _____ is the covering of exchange rate exposure.

19. A _____ is an exchange rate that is agreed to today for some fixed date in the future.

20. _____ and _____ are two other ways to hedge in the foreign exchange market.

21. A free global capital market means that there are few _____ on the movement of capital.

22. An _____ is a less-developed country.

23. A per-unit tax that is levied on an imported good is called a _____.

24. A _____ limits the amount of a foreign good that can be imported.

True-False Questions

1. T   F   Globalization is a rather limited term.

2. T   F   Foreign money is called the exchange rate.

3. T   F   The exchange rate is simply the price of one currency in terms of another.

4. T   F   The exchange rate at any one point in time is the forward exchange rate.

5. T   F   The exchange rate is determined by demand and supply.

6. T   F   The demand for a foreign currency represents the demand for that country's goods, services, and financial assets.

7. T   F   Countries adopting the dollar as their domestic currency are doing a currency swap.

8. T   F   The law of one price is the foundation of purchasing power parity.

9. T   F   When you invest in a foreign country, you must take into account exchange rate changes when you determine your rate of return.

10. T   F   Interest rate parity assumes that capital is not very mobile between countries.

11. T   F   Arbitrage is what makes the law of one price effective.

12. T   F   Arbitrage takes place when the difference between two prices is only due to transportation costs.

13. T   F   Balance sheet exposure can be minimized by having many different branches in many different countries.

14. T   F   Balance sheet exposure can be minimized by limiting the amount of business you do abroad.

15. T   F   Market-based exposure is faced by firms that have no foreign branches.

16. T   F   Firms that source domestically do not need to worry about exchange rate risk.

17. T   F   A firm can cover its exchange rate exposure by hedging.

18. T F Foreign exchange forwards and futures do the same thing and are structured in the same way.

19. T F You should buy a foreign exchange put if you are worried about devaluation.

20. T F Capital is free, to a very large degree, to move between countries.

21. T F The Japanese system of Keiretsu is very flexible.

22. T F A tariff is a tax.

23. T F People argue for trade barriers over a concern for national defense.

24. T F An emerging market is a new marketing scheme.

Multiple-Choice Questions

1. Globalization
    a. is very limited in its meaning.
    b. means many different things.
    c. is the homogenization of everything.
    d. is really not a problem in today's economy.

2. An exchange rate is
    a. the price of one currency in terms of another.
    b. the discount given on a zero coupon bond.
    c. usually determined by government edict.
    d. is the price of one currency in terms of purchasing power.

3. If the dollar depreciated with respect to the pesos
    a. each dollar can buy more pesos.
    b. each dollar can buy the same amount of pesos.
    c. each dollar will buy fewer pesos.
    d. Mexican goods will become less expensive in terms of dollars.

4. The currency of India is the
    a. rupee.
    b. rial.
    c. punt.
    d. yen.

5. The currency of El Salvador is the
    a. peso.
    b. dollar.
    c. lira.
    d. yuan.

6. If the demand for French wines increases
    a. the demand for dollars will rise.
    b. the supply of dollars will fall.
    c. the demand for French francs will rise.
    d. the franc will depreciate.

7. The practice where a nation adopts the U.S. dollar as its currency and essentially eliminates it domestic currency as legal tender is called
   a. transmigration.
   b. conversion.
   c. nationalism.
   d. dollarization.

8. Arbitrage is
   a. buying and selling in anticipation of a price difference.
   b. is only done in foreign exchange markets.
   c. violates the law of one price.
   d. is the buying and selling due to a current price difference.

9. If a price difference for a good in two different locations is equal to the transportation costs between the two locations,
   a. arbitrage will occur.
   b. arbitrage will not occur.
   c. speculation will break out.
   d. the exchange rate is not in equilibrium.

10. The foundation of purchasing power parity
    a. are transaction costs.
    b. is that trade barriers can advance national interests.
    c. is the law of one price.
    d. is found in the global capital market.

11. The foundation of interest rate parity
    a. are transaction costs.
    b. is that trade barriers can advance national interests.
    c. is the law of one price.
    d. is found in the global capital market.

12. Individuals who have invested in a foreign country
    a. need to include exchange rate considerations when calculating their rate of return.
    b. do not need to include exchange rate factors when calculating their rate of return.
    c. need to acknowledge that capital is not mobile between countries.
    d. do not need to have a common currency to make decisions.

13. The return on a bond held in a foreign country will increase if the exchange rate
    a. depreciates.
    b. appreciates.
    c. rolls over.
    d. is held constant with a foreign exchange option.

14. Financial exposure
    a. is the amount gambled.
    b. is equal to a currency option held to maturity.
    c. is equal to the expected value of the return.
    d. is the amount at risk.

15. Companies face exchange rate exposure
    a. through their balance sheets.
    b. through their income statements.
    c. through their product markets.
    d. through all of these things.

16. Market-based exposure can be minimized by
    a. not having foreign branches.
    b. not competing in a global market.
    c. by not selling in the retail market.
    d. by buying a foreign exchange call option.

17. A hedge can be made with
    a. a forward market transaction.
    b. a foreign exchange option.
    c. a currency future.
    d. all of the above.

18. Depreciation can be hedged by
    a. buying a call.
    b. buying a put.
    c. selling a call.
    d. selling on the spot market.

19. When would a preference for an option be appropriate?
    a. When volatility is low.
    b. When the exchange rate will depreciate.
    c. When volatility is high.
    d. When the exchange rate will appreciate.

20. In today's economy, the movement of capital is
    a. restricted.
    b. promoted by Keiretsu banks.
    c. pretty much unrestricted.
    d. only through arbitrage and hedging.

21. A tax on an import is a
    a. quota.
    b. tariff.
    c. hedge.
    d. a sure way to raise revenue for the government.

22. A limit on imports is
    a. a quota.
    b. a tariff.
    c. a hedge.
    d. a sure way to raise revenue for the government.

23. A tariff will raise revenue for the government if the demand for the product is
    a. inelastic.
    b. elastic.
    c. of unit elasticity.
    d. downward sloping.

24. Trade barriers are justified on the basis of
    a. national defense.
    b. protecting jobs.
    c. helping new industries.
    d. all of the above.

Short-Answer Questions

1. What is globalization?

2. Where does an exchange rate come from?

3. What is the difference between a spot and a forward exchange rate?

4. How are exchange rates determined?

5. What does the demand for a nation's currency represent?

6. What is dollarization?

7. Why would a particular product sell for the same price regardless of the market's location?

8. What is purchasing power parity?

9. What is interest rate parity?

10. How is a company exposed to exchange rate risk?

11. What determines the extent of market-based exposure?

12. What is the purpose of hedging?

13. What tools are available for hedging in the foreign exchange market?

14. What is the difference between a foreign exchange forward and a currency future?

15. What does it mean that the capital market is global?

16. What was a structural problem in the Japanese economy that became apparent with the Asian crisis of the 1990s?

17. What are some arguments for the use of tariffs and quotas?

Applications and Problems

1. Why does a foreign exchange call option protect someone from depreciation?

2. What is the difference between arbitrage and speculation?

3. Trade flourished in prisoner of war camps in World War II. Many observers claimed that the prices, usually expressed in cigarettes, of items were the same everywhere across the camps. Why was this the case?

4. Tariffs are used to raise revenue for the government. They usually do not generate much revenue, however. Why?

5. Why is the demand for a currency called a derived demand?

6. Why would a country want to adopt the dollar as its own money?

7. What does the introduction of the Euro mean in terms of the law of one price?

8. The Bush administration levied tariffs on foreign steel. The argument was that U.S. steel companies need time to develop. What does this mean and does it make sense?

9. What is the common element that makes effective the law of one price, purchasing power parity, and interest rate parity?

Extending the Case Study: The Automakers and the Yen

This is a case concerning the role of exchange rates in determining business activity and the call for government action. If you watch CNN for the next week or so, you undoubtedly will hear of another instance where a strong dollar is hurting business. "Things would certainly be better with a weaker dollar. The government needs to help us!" Yet it is usually the case that a weakened dollar did not help solve the problem.

a. If a weak dollar does not help, then where is the problem? Where should we look first?

b. Can you restate the case without using the foreign exchange market?

c. Given your answer to b., what is probably the real problem when the dollar is strong, especially over a long period of time?

ANSWERS TO ACTIVE REVIEW QUESTIONS

Completion Questions

1. Globalization
2. foreign exchange
3. exchange rate
4. spot
5. quantity demanded of a currency, quantity supplied of a currency
6. demand, supply
7. fixed exchange rate
8. dollarization
9. law of one price
10. purchasing power parity
11. arbitrage
12. price differences
13. exchange rate risk
14. Interest rate parity
15. exposure
16. balance sheet exposure, market-based exposure
17. forward market
18. Hedging

19. forward rate
20. Currency futures, foreign exchange options
21. restrictions
22. emerging market
23. tariff
24. quota

True-False Questions

1.	False	2.	False	3.	True
4.	False	5.	True	6.	True
7.	False	8.	True	9.	True
10.	False	11.	True	12.	False
13.	False	14.	True	15.	True
16.	False	17.	True	18.	False
19.	False	20.	True	21.	False
22.	True	23.	True	24.	False

Multiple-Choice Questions

1.	b	2.	a	3.	c
4.	a	5.	b	6.	c
7.	d	8.	d	9.	b
10.	c	11.	c	12.	a
13.	a	14.	d	15.	d
16.	b	17.	d	18.	a
19.	c	20.	c	21.	b
22.	a	23.	a	24.	d

Short-Answer Questions

1. Globalization refers to cross border activities as well as borderless transactions; the location of a manufacturing facility in more than one country; the sale of goods and services in several nations, and the acquisition of resources from many nations.
2. An exchange rate is the price of one currency in terms of another. It is determined on the foreign exchange market.
3. The spot rate is the exchange rate at any point in time. A forward rate is an exchange rate that is agreed to today but which represents a future exchange rate at a unique point in time.

4. Exchange rates are determined in a market by traditional market prices. An equilibrium exchange rate is determined where the quantity demanded of a currency equals the quantity supplied.

5. The demand for a nation's currency represents a demand for the goods and services and financial assets of that country.

6. Dollarization occurs when a country adopts the U.S. dollar as it currency and essentially eliminates its domestic currency as legal tender.

7. This is the outcome of the law of one price. This also assumes that transportation costs and transactions costs are zero. The law of one price holds due to arbitrage.

8. Purchasing power parity argues that in the absence of trade impediments, all tradable goods must sell at the same price everywhere, allowing for transportation costs.

9. Interest rate parity is the law of one price with respect to financial assets. The interest rate or rate of return on an identical financial asset will be the same when measured in the domestic currency.

10. A company can be exposed to exchange rate risk through balance sheet exposure or through market-based exposure.

11. Market-based exposure is largely determined by the global extent of a firm's business activities.

12. The purpose of hedging is to reduce the exposure to exchange rate risk.

13. Various tools are available. There is the forward market, currency futures, and foreign exchange options.

14. Forwards are for any amount while a future is set out in standard contracts. Futures are also standardized by date. The forward market is over the telephone and telex while futures are traded on organized exchanges.

15. This means that the movement of capital is not limited by the boundaries of nations. Capital is free to move to its most valued use regardless of where that is.

16. Banks guaranteed all loans to businesses. Business loans were secured by large industrial groups, called Keiretsu. A bank belonged to each Keiretsu. These arrangements made it very difficult for Japan to compete on a global capital market.

17. First, there is the argument that they save jobs by limiting competition from abroad. Next, national defense reasons are also cited. It is also argued that new or emerging industries need protection from more established foreign competitors.

Applications and Problems

1. An option can be used to protect against devaluation. If you need foreign exchange in the future and believe that the dollar will depreciate, you can buy an option that gives you the right, not the obligation, to buy a foreign currency at an agreed to price over some period of time. So, an option lets you lock in a future exchange rate. If things do not come to pass, you simply do not exercise the option.

2. Arbitrage is the simultaneous buying and selling of a product to take advantage of an existing price difference. Speculation is the buying and holding of a product in hopes of taking advantage of a possible future price change.

3. Given that prisoners had little to do, they engaged in arbitrage. They would move goods from low-price parts of a P.O.W. camp to high-price areas.

4. The ability to raise revenue with a tariff depends on the elasticity of demand. A tariff raises the price of an imported good. Consumers, when faced with a tariff, will move toward substitute goods, if they are available. If they are not available, consumers must buy the

imported good and pay the tariff. So the more elastic the demand, the more difficult it is to raise revenue by using a tariff. The lesson of the question is that people always find substitutes.

5. A foreign currency is not demanded because it is pretty or because it tastes good. It is demanded because it is needed to buy something else. Therefore, the demand for the other good creates the demand for the currency.

6. A country might adopt the dollar if it is dissatisfied with the management of its own money by its central bank. It would also bring stability to a developing country's financial system.

7. The Euro should promote the working of the law of one price. It is hoped that transaction costs in trade in Europe are reduced, given that currency exchanges are no longer needed. Also, the introduction of the Euro marked the reduction in trade barriers between countries in the European Union.

8. This is one of the arguments for tariffs and quotas. Trade barriers will give the developing industry time to get off its feet and be able to compete. This argument is also named the infant industry argument. The problem is that infants never grow up. It is silly to claim that the steel industry in the United States needs time to grow up. It is already old. The move was probably motivated by politics.

9. The common element is the free movement of goods and capital. Mobility is the key to making these things effective.

ANSWERS TO CASE STUDY QUESTIONS

Extending the Case Study: The Automakers and the Yen

a. It is probably the case that the problems are internal to the business. Changes in the exchange rate can certainly affect a business. They also might aggravate other problems. If the exchange rate changes in a more favorable direction and the problems do not go away, then the source of the problems is internal.

b. "A lower-priced seller has entered our market. We need help! They need to be taxed or their costs increased so the playing field is level for everyone."

c. The possible problem is that American automakers did not have a product that added enough value to warrant the higher price. One of the recurring themes of this text is that successful firms add value.

CHAPTER 15

Government and Business

CHAPTER OVERVIEW

Managers operate in many different environments. In the internal environment of the enterprise itself, they structure production, monitor inputs, and control costs. Simultaneously, in the external environment, they operate in input and output markets, design strategies, and react to those of rivals. At all times, the goal of adding value offers guidance to all decisions managers must make regardless of the setting in which they are made.

In these environments, many variables are controllable. However, some are not. A major source of these uncontrollable factors is government. Through anti-trust policies and regulation (both economic and social) all layers of government affect both environments in which managers operate. While government rules often place constraints on decision making, there are times that they can be used as a framework for strategic behavior. The purpose of this chapter is to present an overview of the interaction between government and business.

KEY CONCEPTS FOR REVIEW

Herfindahl-Hirschman Index, HHI	**rule of reason**
per se rule	**natural monopoly**
rent-seeking	**anti-trust policy**
consumer surplus	**economic regulation**
social regulation	

ACTIVE REVIEW

Completion Questions

1. Government affects business through _____ and _____.

2. The majority of anti-trust policy may be found in the _____, _____, and _____.

3. In a competitive market, _____ is maximized.

4. A monopoly is able to reduce the _____ in the market.

5. The _____ is used to measure market concentration.

6. Generally speaking, guidelines suggest that markets must be _____ and that dominant firms can resist pressures to _____ before receiving government attention.

7. Prior to 1914, courts used the _____ to judge a firm's intent. Afterwards, courts used a _____.

8. The _____ of anti-trust laws is often left to the interpretation of a presidential administration.

9. Anti-trust policy is aimed at creating a _____.

10. Competitive strategy says that a firm must develop a _____ that has value in the market place.

11. Competitive strategies can often be seen as _____ by the government.

12. Private anti-trust law suits often represent a _____ for changing the behavior of a _____.

13. A firm is _____ when it sells in a foreign market at a price below its average variable costs.

14. WTO stands for the _____.

15. The two categories of regulation are _____ and _____.

16. A _____ arises when there are extremely large _____ ending in one firm supplying the entire market.

17. Regulatory bureaus determine the rate of a natural monopoly by adding to average costs a _____.

18. The area of the most growth in the business-government interface, is in _____.

19. _____ refers to the use of resources to obtain a transfer of wealth from one group to another.

20. Rent-seeking does not increase _____.

True-False Questions

1. T F   Governments use social regulation to restrict business decision making.

2. T F   Regulation is used to "level the playing field."

3. T F   Anti-trust policy is implemented by the Federal Reserve System.

4. T F   Consumer surplus is the difference between what a consumer is willing and able to pay for a product and the market price.

5. T F   The Herfindahl-Hirschmann Index is used to measure market concentration.

6. T F   The per se rule is simply an application of the rule of reason.

7. T F   Anti-trust policy is implemented by the FTC.

8. T F   Anti-trust policy is pretty consistent among all industrialized nations.

9. T F   Dumping is selling in a foreign country at a price below average total costs.

10. T F   The enforcement of dumping laws does not have an effect on the flow of goods between nations.

11. T F   A form of economic regulation is the setting of the price that a natural monopoly can charge.

12. T F   Natural monopolies result from extremely large economies of scale.

13. T F   Social regulation is applied on a per-case basis.

14. T F   Cost-benefit analysis should be used to analyze the usefulness of social regulation.

15. T F   Social regulation cannot be used as corporate strategy.

16. T F   Rent-seeking creates no output.

Multiple-Choice Questions

1. Government uses which of the following to influence business decision making?
    a. regulation.
    b. anti-trust policy.
    c. the FTC.
    d. the Department of Justice.
    e. all of the above.

2. Anti-trust policy is designed to
    a. prevent all merger activity.
    b. level the playing field.
    c. resurface the ice.
    d. set the price of a natural monopoly.

3. Large firms tend to have
    a. more devious managers.
    b. smaller HHIs.
    c. more market power.
    d. less market power.

4. Monopolies tend to
    a. reduce consumer surplus.
    b. increase consumer surplus.
    c. lower prices.
    d. maintain their barriers for free.

5. The HHI
    a. is a measure of price fixing.
    b. is a measure of market concentration.
    c. is a measure of consumer surplus.
    d. is a strategic tool for utilities.

6. The court rule based on demonstration rather than on appearance is
    a. the rule of reason.
    b. the per se rule.
    c. the level playing field rule.
    d. the golden rule.

7. The court rule based on appearance rather than on demonstration is
    a. the rule of reason.
    b. the per se rule
    c. the golden rule.
    d. the MR=MC rule.

8. Anti-trust laws can be broken by
    a. sharing computers to process airline registrations.
    b. talking to competitors.
    c. exchanging information with rivals.
    d. all of the above.

9. Selling in a foreign market at below average variable cost is called
    a. the rule of reason.
    b. maximizing profits.
    c. dumping.
    d. price fixing.

10. Dumping complaints are trade barriers just like
    a. tariffs.
    b. quotas.
    c. taxes on foreign goods.
    d. all of the above.

11. Economic regulation of a natural monopoly is in the form of
    a. setting a price they can charge.
    b. limiting their market.
    c. requiring pollution equipment.
    d. leveling the playing field.

12. The price that regulators try to set for a natural monopoly is where
    a. MC=ATC.
    b. MC=MR.
    c. MC=Demand.
    d. Q=MR.

13. Social regulation is generally applied to
    a. the largest firms in the market.
    b. all firms.
    c. only natural monopolies.
    d. only foreign firms.

14. Social regulation can serve
    a. as a barrier to entry.
    b. as a strategic asset.
    c. to increase the welfare of a special interest group.
    d. all of the above.

15. Using government to redistribute wealth from one group to another is called
    a. rent-seeking.
    b. social regulation.
    c. the per se rule.
    d. a level playing field.

Short-Answer Questions

1. What are the ways government affects business decision making?

2. In general, what is anti-trust policy?

3. What is consumer surplus and what happens to it when a market is monopolized?

4. What does the government use to measure the control a firm has over its market?

5. What is the rule of reason?

6. What is a per se rule?

7. What is the purpose of anti-trust policy?

8. Can anti-trust policy be used as a business strategy?

9. What is dumping?

10. What are the types of regulation?

11. What is the general form of economic regulation?

12. How does economic regulation attempt to control the price of a natural monopoly?

13. What is the general motivation for social regulation?

14. How would an economist determine whether or not social regulation should exist?

15. What is rent-seeking?

Applications and Problems

1. Does the concentration of a market or limits on entry matter more in judging a merger?

2. In many instances, it is argued that dumping goes on for a long period of time. Does this make sense? Do shareholders have anything to do with your answer?

3. What determines the value of rent-seeking activity?

4. It is argued that monopolies harm the economy. What ways can you think of? Hint: Try to get at least three.

Extending the Case Study: Microsoft

There is nothing in the law that says that a company cannot be big. There is also nothing in the law that says a firm cannot end up being a monopolist by simply supplying the best added value on the market. Problems arise if market power is used in anti-competitive ways. The Microsoft case will probably be used for years by those attempting to find where the line is between an effective competitor and an opportunistic monopolist.

a. How does a firm know what is appropriate market behavior? How does the government know what is inappropriate behavior?

b. Can you think of an argument supporting allowing a monopoly operating system like Microsoft's Windows?

c. In addition to the bundling of the browser issue, in what other ways would a single operating system be a barrier to entry?

d. What are all of Microsoft's moves attempting to do?

ANSWERS TO ACTIVE REVIEW QUESTIONS

Completion Questions

1. anti-trust policy, regulation
2. Sherman, Clayton, Federal Trade Act
3. consumer surplus
4. consumer surplus
5. Herfindahl-Hirschman Index
6. concentrated, lower prices
7. rule of reason, per se rule
8. enforcement
9. level playing field
10. distinctive capability
11. anti-competitive
12. strategy, rival
13. dumping
14. World Trade Organization
15. economic, social
16. natural monopoly, economies of scale
17. fair rate of return on capital
18. social regulation
19. Rent-seeking
20. output

True-False Questions

1.	True	2.	False	3.	False
4.	True	5.	True	6.	False
7.	True	8.	False	9.	True
10.	False	11.	True	12.	True
13.	False	14.	True	15.	False
16.	True				

Multiple-Choice Questions

1.	e	2.	b	3.	c
4.	a	5.	b	6.	a
7.	b	8.	d	9.	c
10.	d	11.	a	12.	c
13.	b	14.	d	15.	a

Short-Answer Questions

1. The government uses regulations and anti-trust policy to affect business decision making.
2. Anti-trust policy attempts to address anti-competitive practices in which businesses might engage.
3. Consumer surplus represent benefits that consumers receive for which they did not pay. It is represented by the area below the demand curve but above the price line. Consumer surplus is maximized in competitive markets. It is reduced and possibly turned into profit for the monopolist.
4. It uses the Herfindahl-Hirschmann Index. The larger the HHI, the more concentrated is the market in the hands of a few firms. Mergers that increase the HHI more than 100 points will be examined closely by the FTC.
5. The rule of reason guided judicial enforcement of anti-trust laws. Just being a monopoly was not enough. Actions need to be unfair, anti-competitive, and demonstrated.
6. This is a judicial guide for anti-trust enforcement. The mere existence of activities was illegal.
7. The purpose is to create a level playing field.
8. Certainly. An private anti-trust suit can be brought to try to change the behavior of a rival.
9. Dumping is usually described as a foreign rival selling at a price below average variable costs.
10. There is economic and social regulation.

11. The general form of economic regulation is to control the price of a natural monopoly.
12. The price of a natural monopoly is set level equal to average accounting costs plus a fair rate of return for capital.
13. The general motivation is to protect the public from harmful business practices or from the harmful effects resulting from business activity.
14. An economist would use cost-benefit analysis. It is often the case that regulation benefits special interests and not the public.
15. Rent-seeking refers to the use of resources to obtain a transfer of wealth from one group to another. It is often used by firms in a market to block the entry of others.

Applications and Problems

1. Recall that the first thing consumers do when a price increases is to look for a substitute good. Also, recall that economic profits attract copycats. Just because a merger may increase the concentration of a market as judged by the HHI, it does not necessarily mean that it is more difficult for a new rival to enter. Also, just because a market is concentrated by merger activity does not mean that the consumer has few choices. For example, if two newspapers merge, one must consider the appropriate market before judging the merger. The market may be for "information services." If this is the case, then one must also consider internet access, competition among television new services, etc., while judging the merger of the two papers.
2. The goal of management should be to add value. In one way, this means that price should be greater than average total costs. Consistently selling below average variable costs means that the managers of the dumping firm are not adding value, at least in the market where the dumping is occurring. While dumping may be a strategic move, it makes little sense as a long-run policy.
3. The value of rent-seeking activity should be the value of economic profit it might generate. Resources used to seek rents have alternative uses. Therefore, rent-seeking needs to be worth more than the value of these opportunity costs.
4. Monopolies reduce consumer surplus. This is done by raising price and by lowering output. So the consumer is worse off by (1) a higher price and (2) by less output. The consumer is also worse off in that a monopoly needs to maintain its single seller position. It must continue to seek rents and protect its barrier. These activities use resources that could be used to produce other goods. Thus, (3) resources are used by the monopolist that produce nothing of value for the market.

ANSWERS TO CASE STUDY QUESTIONS

Extending the Case Study: Microsoft

a. While illegal practices may be found in statute (written law), most practices are found in the precedent of case law. This is to say, there is the knowledge of what others have done in the past—what was allowed and what was not allowed. The government essentially does the same thing. Given the newness of the computer and technology industries, some have argued that Microsoft was chosen to begin testing the boundaries for legal and illegal behavior in the primer industry of the new economy. Based on the behavior or prices, the market seemed very competitive. Yet some of Microsoft's strategies seemed to seek an unfair advantage.

The Microsoft case began finding where the lines will be drawn.

b. Given the widespread use of desktop and laptop personal computers, one could argue that economic efficiency is promoted if people don't have to learn a new operating system every time they sit down in front of a different computer. They can simply operate programs. Therefore, giving Windows a monopoly would save time and money in the production of goods and services.

c. Software designers must know the codes that make up the operating system. By controlling the operating system, Microsoft can possibly control which software applications become available for consumers. So, by having a proprietary system, Microsoft can block entry into the market for software.

d. Microsoft is attempting to protect its value added and prevent its duplication. Microsoft is doing what any other business would do if it were in the same market position.

CHAPTER 16

Strategy and Management

CHAPTER OVERVIEW

This chapter attempts to put it all together. How does one develop an effective corporate strategy? It has been argued in the text from the beginning that economic thinking can be invaluable to a manager. An economic approach to thinking recognizes that every decision, while having benefits, also has costs. It is not effective strategy to be all things to all people. Decision makers must first define their positions. To whom are they selling and in what market? Who are the rivals? The most likely area for success will be in those places that add the most value. To extend this into the long run, this additional value should be very costly for rivals to imitate. This can be accomplished through a strategic audit. Next, decision makers need to see the relationship between technical production decisions and the behavior of costs. They need to understand the supply chain. Within this is the appropriate incentive system for all resources.

KEY CONCEPTS FOR REVIEW

strategic audit   strategic positioning

imitation vs. innovation   market boundaries

strategic assets   supply chain management

ACTIVE REVIEW

Completion Questions

1. Management strategy is simply utilizing _____.

2. Successful firms _____.

3. Incumbent firms often become _____ and stop looking for opportunities.

4. In a _____ a firm identifies and defines its distinctive capabilities, strategic assets, potential markets, and sustainable advantages.

5. A business can define itself by looking at _____, _____, and _____.

6. Boundaries are drawn where the _____ of stretching them equals the _____.

7. Every customer exacts an _____.

8. A market boundary is often defined by determining how customers obtain _____ in the market.

9. A _____ is something of value that enables the firm to create a distinctive position.

10. There is no free _____.

True-False Questions

1. T F   A strategic position is not unique.

2. T F   To be successful, a firm needs to copy others.

3. T F   Innovative firms are generally small and new to the market.

4. T F   "Breaking the rules" should be subject to cost-benefit analysis.

5. T F   The first step in a strategic audit is to identify the supply chain.

6. T F   A business can be defined around a product, core competency, and/or a customer function.

7. T F   Market boundaries are determined by sunk costs.

8. T F   Supply chain management is identified by the vertical relationships of a firm.

9. T F   A strategic asset can create a distinctive position.

10. T F   Corporate culture raises costs.

Multiple-Choice Questions

1. A strategic position
   a. should be duplicative.
   b. is unique.
   c. can be imitated quickly.
   d. is not subject to changes in consumer tastes.

2. To be successful a company
   a. must create and exploit a unique strategic position.
   b. must copy others.
   c. should seek government protection.
   d. should control the entire supply chain.

3. Most companies that innovate
   a. have large research departments.
   b. do so with patents.
   c. are small.
   d. are not thinking strategically.

4. A strategic revolutionary
   a. breaks rules.
   b. follows rules.
   c. copies others.
   d. is a contrarian.

5. A strategic audit
   a. defines distinctive capabilities.
   b. identifies markets.
   c. identifies strategic assets.
   d. does all of the above.

6. A business can be defined
   a. in whatever form a firm wants.
   b. by telling customers what they want.
   c. around a product.
   d. only after anti-trust considerations are addressed.

7. Boundaries may be defined around
   a. products.
   b. consumers.
   c. core competencies.
   d. all of the above.

8. In a competitive market
   a. suppliers are price-makers.
   b. a firm can acquire products from any number of suppliers.
   c. the supply chain is horizontal.
   d. supply chain management is not necessary.

9. For an asset to be valuable
   a. it can be copied.
   b. it should have substitutes
   c. it must be rare.
   d. it needs complementary products.

10. Culture must be consistent with
    a. corporate architecture.
    b. price elasticity of demand.
    c. legal requirements.
    d. an inverted fit.

Short-Answer Questions

1. What is strategy?

2. What does it mean to use strategic positioning?

3. What is a strategic revolutionary?

4. What is a strategic audit?

5. What are various ways to define a market boundary?

6. Supply chain management is attempting to identify what type of relationships.

7. What do strategic assets do?

8. What determines a firm's "fit?"

Applications and Problems

1. It is noted in the text that many established firms stop looking for the new and creative avenue—"If it ain't broke, don't fix it" sort of thing. Why? What might they be confusing? Hint: Think in terms of costs.

2. Many of the remaining dot.com firms were the first ones in the market. What is this telling you about the nature of the marketplace?

3. Why does success only last about five years?

4. What did the internet allow new firms to do compared to pre-internet start-ups? Was this a blessing or a curse?

Extending the Case Study: Edward Jones Brokerage

Edward Jones Brokerage identified a niche and served it. Apparently, based on the reported profitability, the entrepreneurial brokers add value. While the case analysis is pretty complete a few questions remain unanswered.

a. What type of price elasticity of demand does Edward Jones Brokerage face? Support your answer.

b. Did they appeal to stock traders or investors?

c. How would you have defined their market?

ANSWERS TO ACTIVE REVIEW QUESTIONS

Completion Questions

1. the economic way of thinking
2. add value
3. complacent
4. strategic audit
5. products, customer function, core competencies
6. marginal benefit, marginal cost
7. opportunity cost
8. information
9. strategic asset
10. lunch

True-False Questions

1. False   2. False   3. True
4. True   5. False   6. True
7. False   8. True   9. True
10. False

Multiple-Choice Questions

1. b   2. a   3. c
4. a   5. d   6. c
7. d   8. b   9. c
10. a

Short-Answer Questions

1. Strategy is simply utilizing the economic way of thinking.
2. This is finding and exploiting a unique position in a market.
3. A strategic revolutionary is a firm that "breaks all the rules" of the game. This is done by attempting to stop being complacent.
4. A strategic audit is when a firm tries to define and identify its distinctive capabilities and strategic assets, the market or markets they are in, and the extent to which the have sustainable competitive advantages.
5. Market boundaries may be defined by the product produced, the customer function served, or by the portfolio of core competencies.

6. Supply chain management attempts to identify the vertical relationships a firm possesses.
7. Strategic assets are things that are valuable to the firm that enable it to be distinctive.
8. A fit is determined by the firm's architecture and its strategy. It is also defined by the incentive system used to motivate resources.

Applications and Problems

1. Many firms feel that they have too much money tied up in what they are currently doing to innovate. New activities do not necessarily mean that old ones lose all their value, however. The cost of doing something new is the marginal cost and not all previous sunk costs.
2. This is telling you that entry into the internet was easy and that the value added by the first firms was easily copied. As such, economic profits did not last long. The most recent firms to enter failed to see that they could not add value.
3. Success is fleeting because it attracts others. If a firm cannot protect its strategic position, it must find a new one if it is to survive.
4. The internet allowed new start-ups to become instantly big. Pre-internet firms grew more slowly and may have had an easier time adjusting to being big. Given the wide and easy access of the internet, new start-ups may have had to face the issues of being big (like effective supply chain management) to soon in their development. As such, the internet may have been a curse and not a total blessing.

ANSWERS TO CASE STUDY QUESTIONS

Extending the Case Study: Edward Jones Brokerage

a. Edward Jones Brokerage probably faced a relatively inelastic demand. This is apparent from the fact that they did not need to face the services offered by internet trading firms. Those firms competed simply on the basis of price. This suggests that the typical Edward Jones client was probably not very price sensitive.
b. They appealed to investors. Notice that they did not grow by offering short-term trading services.
c. The are in financial services and information marketing. They marketed the products of other companies rather than having their own. They also offered one type of advice—long term-investment strategies.